McGRAW-HILL EDUCATION CLASSICS

EDWARD H. REISNER, *General Editor*

THE CONDUCT OF THE SCHOOLS

OF

JEAN-BAPTISTE DE LA SALLE

McGRAW-HILL EDUCATION CLASSICS

EDWARD H. REISNER, *General Editor*

Early Protestant Educators
  Edited by FREDERICK EBY

Comenius
  Edited by M. W. KEATINGE

French Liberalism and Education in the Eighteenth Century
  Edited by F. DE LA FONTAINERIE

Thomas Jefferson and Education in a Republic
  Edited by CHARLES FLINN ARROWOOD

Pestalozzi
  Edited by LEWIS FLINT ANDERSON

Reports on European Education
  Edited by EDGAR W. KNIGHT

Henry Barnard on Education
  Edited by JOHN S. BRUBACHER

Pioneers of Women's Education
  Edited by WILLYSTINE GOODSELL

Educational Views of Benjamin Franklin
  Edited by THOMAS WOODY

St. Ignatius and the Ratio Studiorum
  Edited by EDWARD A. FITZPATRICK

The Conduct of the Schools of Jean-Baptiste de la Salle
  Edited by F. DE LA FONTAINERIE

THE
CONDUCT OF THE SCHOOLS
OF
JEAN-BAPTISTE DE LA SALLE

Translation and Introduction

by

F. DE LA FONTAINERIE

McGRAW-HILL BOOK COMPANY, INC.

NEW YORK AND LONDON

1935

Reprinted with permission of the publisher

in a limited edition

by St. Mary's College Press, Winona, Minn.

1959

PRINTED IN THE UNITED STATES OF AMERICA

TO

BROTHER ELIPHUS JOHN F.S.C.

PREFACE

THIS translation of the first printed edition of the *Conduite des écoles* of St. Jean-Baptiste de la Salle, published in Avignon in 1720, has been made from a typescript copy of an exemplar of this edition which is preserved in the archives of the Mother House of the Brothers of the Christian Schools at Lembecq-les-Hal, Belgium.

The copy was graciously presented by Brother Abban-Philippe, Assistant to the Superior General, to Professor Edward H. Reisner of Teachers College, Columbia University, who generously permitted the translator to make use of it. The writer desires to express both to Brother Abban-Philippe and to Professor Reisner his great appreciation of their kindness.

The translation is a faithful rendering into the simplest English possible, without any attempt to improve the style. Where the original is verbose, so is the translation. Alone, occasionally, very long sentences with several subordinate clauses have been separated into shorter sentences for the sake of clearness.

The sources for the brief biography of St. De la Salle and the account of the Institute are: J.-B. Blain, *Vie du Bienheureux Serviteur de Dieu Jean-Baptiste de la Salle,* Paris, 1889. (This is the work of a contemporary of St. De la Salle, and was first published in 1733.) J. Guibert, *Histoire de S. Jean-Baptiste de la Salle,* Paris, 1901. Also by the same author, *Vie de S. Jean-Baptiste de la Salle,* Tours, 1905.

PREFACE

Fernand Laudet, *L'instituteur des instituteurs,* Tours, 1929.
Jules Herment, *Les idées pédagogiques de Saint Jean-Baptiste de la Salle,* Paris, 1932. John William Adamson, *Pioneers of Modern Education, 1600–1700,* Cambridge, 1921. An article on the Brothers of the Christian Schools in the *American Journal of Education,* Vol. III, Hartford, 1858. A similar article in Paul Monroe's *Cyclopedia of Education,* Vol. I, New York, 1911. Mrs. R. F. Wilson, *The Christian Brothers, Their Origin and Their Work,* London, 1883. Articles on St. John Baptist de la Salle and on the Institute of the Brothers of the Christian Schools in the *Catholic Encyclopedia,* Vol. VIII, New York, 1910.

The writer wishes to acknowledge his debt of gratitude to Brother Alfred, lately President of La Salle College, Philadelphia, for not only affording him all the facilities of the college library but even having books especially imported for his use; to Brother E. Louis, the Librarian, for his kindly assistance in making use of this material; to Brother James, Principal of the West Philadelphia Catholic High School for Boys, for the loan of books; and to Brother Eliphus John, the benevolent intermediary through whom all the helpful contacts with the other Brothers were made, to whom it is impossible to acknowledge special obligations, so general and continuous has been his assistance, and to whom in reality the inception of this work is due.

Very sincere thanks are tendered Professor J. A. Meredith of Temple University, Philadelphia, for his kindness in reading the manuscript.

F. de la F.

PHILADELPHIA,
September, 1935.

CONTENTS

CONTENTS

CONTENTS

CONTENTS

PART II

MEANS OF ESTABLISHING AND MAINTAINING ORDER IN THE SCHOOLS

CONTENTS

CONTENTS

LIFE AND WORK
OF
ST. JEAN-BAPTISTE DE LA SALLE

I. EARLY YEARS OF ST. DE LA SALLE

JEAN-BAPTISTE DE LA SALLE, priest, educator, saint, was born in Reims on April 30, 1651. Through his father, Louis de la Salle, and his mother, born Moët de Brouillet, he was related to the most honorable and highly respected families of the province of Champagne. Piety was one of the chief characteristics of the family: two of his brothers, Jacques-Joseph and Louis, became priests; and his sister Marie, a nun.

He seems never to have attended any primary school, though such schools must have been common enough in his neighborhood at that time.* Hence we may infer that his father preferred that he should take the first steps in learning at home. However, this could not continue beyond the age of nine years; for an ordinance of Henri IV (issued in 1600 for the University of Paris but faithfully observed in Reims) forbade that any child over that age should be taught at home.

At the time, there existed in Reims two large colleges offering complete courses: the Jesuit College and the Collège

---

* In this district, between 1686 and 1689, slightly over 49 per cent of the men who married were able to sign the register. F. Buisson, *Dictionnaire de pédagogie,* Part I, Tome I, p. 354, Paris, 1886.

des Bons Enfants. The latter dated from the time of Charle-magne, when ten or twelve poor children, who had been adopted by the Church, were lodged in a former convent while they attended the Cathedral School. These children were called *les bons enfants,* and the name remained attached to the house, which continued to serve as a residence for students until, in 1544, the Cathedral Chapter transferred thither its public schools. Ten years later, when the University of Reims was founded, this school became a part of it.

After a long and honorable career, the Collège des Bons Enfants had, in the seventeenth century, fallen from its high estate—probably because the Jesuits had by their excellent methods caused their college to develop at the expense of that of the university. It was, however, to the Collège des Bons Enfants that Louis de la Salle decided to send his son. His choice may have been due to the fact that he was a member of the magistracy and of the City Council, both of which were the natural protectors of this school. Furthermore, about this time serious efforts to reform it were being made.

Jean-Baptiste entered the Collège des Bons Enfants in 1660, when he was nine years old, and he completed there the entire course of studies. Throughout this time he continued to reside at home. The instruction which he received in the college and the family life which he shared were both imbued with religious spirit and of a nature to foster a vocation to the priesthood. Before he had completed his eleventh year, he felt that he had such a vocation. He informed his parents of his desire and, as he met with no opposition, received the tonsure on March 11, 1662.

In the seventeenth century, it was not extraordinary that a child aged eleven should receive the tonsure. Such an act implied no solemn engagement but merely indicated that the youth had then the intention of dedicating himself at a more mature age to the service of the Church. It probably signified no more than would the conferring of a scholarship upon a possible candidate for holy orders in our time.

The prominence of his family would doubtless have enabled Jean-Baptiste to obtain some important ecclesiastical benefice upon his reception of the tonsure, but he did nothing of the sort. It was not until five years later that a canonicate in the cathedral of Reims was conferred upon him, and apparently through no solicitation on the part of his family. A certain Canon Dozet, Archdeacon of Champagne and Chancellor of the University of Reims, who was related to his family, had watched with interest the progress of the young cleric; and when, on Easter Sunday, 1666, the baccalaureate was conferred upon the latter, he decided to resign his canonicate in favor of the young man. On January 7, 1667, the new Canon was installed, and on March 17 of the following year he took minor orders. He continued his studies at the University, and after receiving the degree of Master of Arts on July 10, 1669, he began the course in theology, which he followed for one year at the University of Reims.

In all France—perhaps in all Europe—the Sorbonne in Paris was the foremost school of theology, and to it came students from all parts. There too went Jean-Baptiste de la Salle in 1670. He resided at the Seminary of St. Sulpice, where he came into contact with some of the most eminent ecclesiastics of the period.

At that time, to many leaders of Christian activities the education of the lower classes seemed to be of paramount importance. Whether out of pity for the masses who swarmed in ignorance and vice or out of fear of the excesses which a populace unrestrained by religious sentiment might commit, the instruction and Christianization of the poor were a constant subject of discussion. As an association for the furtherance of this objective existed at St. Sulpice, it was probably there that Jean-Baptiste became interested in popular education.

Very soon occurred two events which brought about a change in the plans of the young man: in July, 1671, his mother died; and in the following April came the death of his father. As he was the eldest son, Jean-Baptiste felt that he ought to take the place of his father in the household and provide for the education and establishment in life of his brothers and sisters, so he at once returned to Reims.

Canon de la Salle did not permit the new duties that he had assumed to interfere with the obligations of his office. In June, 1672, he received the subdeaconate. Not until 1676 did he receive the deaconate; but in the meanwhile he had continued his theological studies at the University of Reims and had obtained the *licence* toward the end of 1677. On Holy Saturday, April 9, 1678, he was ordained priest. After three more years of study at the University, the doctorate was conferred upon him.

Here ends what may be considered the first period of the life of St. Jean-Baptiste de la Salle: the formative period, of study and of preparation for his lifework—a life and work indeed different from what might have been expected for a Canon of the Cathedral Chapter, a Doctor of Theology, a member of the aristocracy, a man of considerable wealth.

II. INCEPTION OF THE CHRISTIAN SCHOOLS

Since his return from Paris, Canon de la Salle had had as his spiritual director Canon Nicolas Roland, a man of great energy, much occupied with charitable works. Chief among these was the establishing of schools for girls of the poorer classes and of a congregation of nuns to teach in the schools. As Canon Roland was in poor health, and it seemed that his end was approaching, he decided to make Canon de la Salle his successor in the work. To this end he advised the latter to exchange his canonicate for a parish, as a parish priest would be better able to further such a work. Though the Archbishop refused to permit this, Canon Roland made Canon de la Salle the executor of his will and charged him with the duty of establishing upon a solid basis the principal work of his life: the Congregation of the Sisters of the Holy Child Jesus,* which he had organized in 1670, but for which he had been unable so far to obtain official recognition. To do this was the immediate duty that devolved upon Canon de la Salle. After many efforts he succeeded, and in 1679 letters patent authorizing the congregation were issued.

In the seventeenth century, elementary schools were very general throughout France;† but often in the cities the children of the populace were terribly neglected. Either because they were unable to attend the pay schools or be-

---

* This congregation must not be confused with the Society of the Holy Child Jesus, a congregation of women, likewise dedicated to teaching, founded in England in the nineteenth century, which has several Houses in the United States.

† E. ALLAIN, *L'instruction primaire en France avant la Révolution,* Chap. IV, Paris, 1881.

cause no effort was made to attract them, they remained on the streets, subject to all the vices that ignorance and vagabondage engender. It is true that there were charity schools, but they were not sufficiently numerous. Popular education was awaiting a reformation and an organizer.

In Rouen there were two devoted persons who were working to establish free schools. One of these was Father Barré, a Franciscan who had organized a teaching congregation of women; the other was Mme de Maillefer, a lady who devoted her time and wealth to the maintenance of teachers in charity schools. As she had originally come from Reims and wished to afford her native city the benefits of popular education, she had sent to Canon Roland the first religious of the Congregation of the Holy Child. Early in 1679, she decided to establish in Reims charity schools for boys also. For this purpose, she chose a devoted man who, under the name of Brother Gabriel, had for the previous twenty-seven years directed the charity schools in Rouen. His name was Adrien Nyel, and he was fifty-five years old. With the simplicity of a child, he set out on the promise of Mme de Maillefer to provide him a yearly income of three hundred livres.*

Upon his arrival in Reims, Adrien Nyel presented himself to the Superior of the Congregation of the Holy Child. She was favorably impressed and willing to give her assistance. In her opinion, Nyel should consult Canon de la Salle. The Canon received him with his usual benevolence and took him to lodge in his own home. This was the first

* The livre was of about the same value as the gold franc, which replaced it in 1795.

step toward the establishment of the Institute of the Brothers of the Christian Schools.

After many conferences with those priests in the city who were most zealous in the cause of popular education, a meeting was held in the house of the Canon, and it was decided to follow his idea and place the schools under the protection of a parish priest. The masters of the pay schools were very tenacious of their privileges and suffered only parish priests to open free schools and then for the poor children of their own parishes only. An arrangement was made with the pastor of the parish of St. Maurice, and a school was opened on April 16, 1679, which may be rightly considered the first school of the Christian Brothers. In this school, children who up to that time had been left to vagrancy and evil-doing were taught reading, arithmetic, Christian Doctrine, and deportment.

The new school attracted such favorable attention that a devout and wealthy widow, Mme Lévêque de Croyère, sent for Canon de la Salle and requested him to establish a second school in her own parish of St. Jacques, which she agreed to endow with an annual income of five hundred livres. This lady died before the project could be realized, but she had made provision for the promised income, which was regularly paid. In the meanwhile, Adrien Nyel had been recruiting aids, and as three had offered themselves, it was possible to open the school in the parish of St. Jacques in September, 1679. There were now five teachers altogether who continued to live in the house of the parish priest of St. Maurice.

Canon de la Salle began to perceive that Nyel, in spite

of his many good qualities, was not capable of governing a community; and his young teachers, whom no previous training had prepared to be self-sufficient, were suffering the inevitable consequences of lack of guidance. If the charity schools were to continue, something had to be done. Thus, he found it necessary to assume more and more the responsibility of the little community. It seemed that many difficulties would be obviated if the teachers dwelt in a house of their own, where they could follow a more precise routine and observe a more definite rule. Canon de la Salle, therefore, installed them in a house near his own residence.

Adrien Nyel's frequent absences in quest of new teachers for a third school, to be established in the parish of St. Symphorien—the parish in which was situated the house of the teachers—could not fail to have a bad effect upon a group of young men, who, without any special preparation, had undertaken arduous duties and were required to follow a rule similar to that of a religious order. Canon de la Salle, observing this, sought some remedy for the situation. There seemed but one that would really be efficacious: to take the teachers into his own home and share their lives. This was a momentous decision to make. What would people say—his relatives above all—if he received into his home, at his table, men of a condition so inferior to his own? Would he be able to overcome his fastidiousness and lead a life in common with men of the lower class, devoid of the culture to which he had been accustomed all his life? Saints are not exempt from human feelings! Jean-Baptiste de la Salle realized that he had a duty to his family and to his class, and yet there seemed no other solution to the difficulty. In order to bring about the change gradually, he first had the teachers take their meals with him—he was already providing them with food, so it would seem only natural that they should come to his house for their repasts.

During the Easter vacation, the Canon conducted a retreat for the teachers. Every day, for a week, they came to his house at seven o'clock in the morning and remained until after evening prayers. This retreat proved so beneficial that Adrien Nyel urged him to take the teachers to live with him under his direct supervision. The step appeared inevitable and no longer to be postponed. On June 24, 1681, the teachers came to live in the home of their benefactor. It had already seemed extraordinary that a man of Canon de la Salle's position should occupy himself to such an extent with the teachers in the charity schools; but respect for his family and his office had in some degree stifled comment. Not so, however, at this juncture: people of his own class no longer refrained from openly expressing their disapproval. His relatives, greatly annoyed, even accused him of neglecting his brothers and sisters in order to care for his schoolmasters; and they finally took steps to deprive him of the guardianship of his younger brothers who lived with him.

Instead of weakening his resolution, this action, by detaching him from his family and freeing him from social obligations, served only to draw the Canon closer to his chosen work and to his adopted family. The schools made such manifest progress that from various places came requests for teachers. In spite of his reluctance to send out his young recruits until they had been thoroughly trained,

Canon de la Salle felt obliged to provide teachers for four different places outside Reims. The foundations of the Institute of the Brothers of the Christian Schools had been laid.

As there was nothing to retain him in the sumptuous family mansion, which he realized was not a suitable residence for a community of poor schoolmasters, the Canon decided to go with them to a house of their own in a quieter neighborhood. In June, 1682, just one year after the teachers had come to live in his house, he went to live with them in theirs—the first House of the Community. A rule of life was drawn up which left no hour of the day unemployed. Such monastic regularity was not entirely to the liking of a group of young men who had the intention of becoming schoolmasters and not religious; they found it tiresome, the food too simple, their freedom too much restricted. A number of them left the Community. This was a cruel blow for Canon de la Salle, but he soon realized that it was better so. The breaks in the ranks were readily filled by recruits who understood the obligations and willingly assumed them.

There was, however, one grave preoccupation that troubled the minds of the teachers: so long as Canon de la Salle looked after them, so long as they could continue their work, all would be well; but if their valiant director should be taken from them, and their schools should fail, for lack of any other resource they would be destitute. When the Canon heard of this, he strove to dispel their fears by means of words of encouragement. The teachers, however, were obsessed by a thought that they could no longer conceal: "It is easy for you to speak thus; you are a man of means and have a good benefice, whereas we have nothing if our schools should fail." This was a revelation to Jean-Baptiste de la Salle. Far from being offended, he admitted the justice of the observation, and he understood that he would never be able to fulfill his duties as Superior until he had made himself poor like the other members of the Community. He at once determined to resign his canonicate, for he felt that the duties thereof were incompatible with his obligations to the Community. When his project became known, a storm of comment arose: some declared that he had lost his mind; others, that he was only following his natural inclination to rush to extremes.

The Archbishop, who was somewhat prejudiced against Canon de la Salle, refused several times to receive him, but finally did so and authorized him to resign his canonicate in favor of a priest named Faubert, a worthy man but of humble birth. The Canons of the Cathedral were displeased that, without being consulted, they should be expected to receive among them a man of mean social condition; and the members of the De la Salle family were indignant that a benefice which had originally come from a relative should not be transferred to one of the Canon's brothers. However, having obtained the Archbishop's authorization, M. de la Salle persisted in his intention.

There was yet more to be done, for Jean-Baptiste de la Salle had resolved to follow completely the evangelical precept "Go sell what thou hast, and give to the poor." Only the manner of doing it remained to be determined. Soon enlightenment came through the course of events. During the winter of 1684 and most of the following year, poverty and misery were so great that he felt that the opportune moment had come to distribute to the sufferers the wealth that seemed to him superfluous for his purpose in life.

When it came to the actual distribution of his fortune, he did it in as orderly a manner as though he were only the steward of wealth entrusted to him for this purpose. The poor whom he aided he divided into three categories:

The school children who, morning and afternoon, received each a portion of bread.

The bashful and timid poor who were ashamed to avow their poverty were the objects of his greatest solicitude. He watched all who he suspected were in want, and when he found cases that required help, he sent them aid so discreetly that their self-respect was not wounded.

Those who were recognized as objects of charity he assembled in the House of the Community and, after a religious instruction, distributed generous alms.

In this manner his fortune was soon exhausted, and Jean-Baptiste de la Salle had descended to the condition of the poor. His conduct in acting thus was not that of a visionary, of a man lacking in practical wisdom. This is proved by a memorandum found among his papers, which sets forth his reasons in detail and shows that he was guided by a sort of inspired common sense.*

III. The First Assembly of the Institute

It seemed to M. de la Salle that the time had come to unite the teachers in the various schools under his care in a regular religious society. For this purpose, he called together in council the principal teachers in his schools in

* An abridged translation of this memorandum may be found in *The American Journal of Education*, Vol. III, p. 438.

Reims and the Directors of the schools in three neighboring towns. In this assembly, everything concerning the new society was discussed. Every teacher was encouraged to express his views. For fear lest the authority of his words should dominate, the Superior was always the last to speak. A vote was taken before each decision, and the majority vote decided the question.

The first matters to be considered were rules and a constitution. The general opinion was, however, that it was too soon to draw them up in written form; it appeared better to test for a time the existing usages.

The question of food presented no difficulty. It was to be as uniform in all the Houses as possible: a wisely arranged diet which, by its adequacy, would satisfy the demands of health and, by its plainness, the obligations of penance.

It was agreed that some sort of religious garb should be adopted to distinguish the members of the Society from the secular teachers; but the decision concerning details was left to the Superior. The following winter, the teachers, going to and from their schools in snow and rain, badly protected, inspired the pity of the mayor, who advised the Superior to provide each with a *capote,* an ample mantle with loose sleeves, used by the peasants of the province. The Superior adopted it, and for an indoor garb a cassock of black cloth, fastened in front with steel hooks and eyes, such as was at that time worn by priests in certain parts of France. A white neckband and a three-cornered hat completed the costume of a Brother.

This habit at first appeared strange and even drew ridicule upon its wearers. They, undaunted, continued to go their way and by their devotion and their merits made it respected and honored—as it still is. To this day it is the official habit of the "Christian Brothers," and it is worn by them all the world over, at least in their Houses and schools. In some countries, for practical reasons, another costume is worn in public places.

The title "Brothers of the Christian Schools" was chosen for the Society, and it was decided that the members should renounce their original names and be known by a new one with the appellation Brother.

M. de la Salle had for a long time felt that the Brothers ought to pass some time in serious preparation for their work; but, hitherto, he had been obliged to yield to the imperious demands of the moment. He, therefore, established a novitiate in order to provide both religious and pedagogic training. There was also need of educational opportunity for many candidates who were too young to enter the novitiate; for these was created the "Little Novitiate." In this seminary, the lads could undergo a long training which would fit them to enter the regular novitiate.

In spite of the constantly increasing number of Brothers, the Superior could not accede to all the requests for teachers that came from parish priests in the country districts. Not only were there not enough Brothers to supply these demands, but also, the Superior made it a rule never to send fewer than two Brothers to open a school. As a means to satisfy to some extent the need for trained teachers, parish priests, who so desired, could send young men from their own parishes for special training in the methods employed by the Brothers. In this manner was created a training school for future teachers—in other words, a normal school.

M. de la Salle also formed the project of establishing, on the estate of the Duke de Mazarin at Rethel and under his patronage, a school solely for the training of lay teachers; but the Archbishop refused to authorize it, and it was not until fifteen years later, when he was established in Paris, that the project was realized. St. De la Salle established six different normal schools, to one of which, at St. Denis, he even planned to attach a practice school. The idea of creating establishments for training teachers for primary schools has been attributed to the National Convention.* This is a grave error; St. Jean-Baptiste de la Salle established, one hundred years before the Revolution, the earliest professional school for the training of teachers.†

To claim for the National Convention the credit of having established the first normal school cannot be justified on the ground that those founded by St. De la Salle did not have a continued existence. No more did the one founded by the Convention: it was decreed in principle, opened for a few months in 1795, and then ceased to exist. Furthermore, in decreeing the establishment of a "school for the dissemination of uniform teaching in all France," the Convention merely took over a project which had been broached by Louis XV in letters patent of November 21, 1763.‡

* F. Buisson, *op. cit.,* Part I, Tome II, p. 2058.
† *American Journal of Education,* Vol. III, p. 437. F. Laudet, *L'instituteur des instituteurs,* p. 161.
‡ A.-F. Théry, *Histoire de l'éducation en France depuis le cinquième siècle,* Vol. II, p. 190, Paris, 1858.

IV. Establishment of the Institute in Paris

The parish priest of St. Sulpice in Paris proposed to entrust to the Brothers the charity schools of his parish. This proposal greatly pleased M. de la Salle; for, being established in the capital, the Institute would cease to be a mere diocesan institution, dependent for its existence upon successive archiepiscopal administrations, and could attain the autonomy necessary for its complete development. He, therefore, confided the Community in Reims to Brother Henri L'Heureux and, accompanied by two Brothers, set out on foot for Paris in February, 1688.

M. de la Salle and the two Brothers were placed in charge of a parochial charity school in the rue Princesse. They found everything in an appalling state of disorder, which they soon rectified. An injunction was sought against the Superior by the teachers of pay schools, who feared lest the Brothers attract pupils from them. The Brothers were summoned to appear before the Precentor of the Cathedral of Notre Dame, under whose jurisdiction came matters pertaining to schools. The Precentor was a zealous protector of the privileges of the schoolmasters, and he ordered the suppression of the Brothers' schools.

M. de la Salle had such a horror of strife that he was ready to give up the work in Paris rather than appeal against the verdict of the Precentor. The parish priest of St. Sulpice felt that his official rights had been attacked, and he obliged the Superior to present an appeal, accompanied by a written defense of the Institute, to the Parliament of Paris. The verdict was annulled, the Brothers returned to their schools, and the schoolmasters kept the peace for the time being.

Other tribulations were not lacking. The Brothers whom the Superior had brought with him from Reims left the Community, and other defections also occurred in Reims. The Little Novitiate there was so affected that it was thought best to transfer it to Paris in 1690. The difficulties in Reims had all developed after Brother Henri L'Heureux, whom M. de la Salle had left in charge there, had come to Paris, whither he had been called by the Superior. This Brother had governed his Community so successfully that M. de la Salle had selected him to become later the Superior of the Institute, and to this end he desired that he should study theology at the Sorbonne and become a priest. From this fact it would appear that M. de la Salle, although he seems to have already determined that the various Communities should be governed by Brothers, still felt that the Superior of the whole Institute should be a priest. This is easy to comprehend. At a time when the clergy were so powerful and tenacious of their rights and privileges, it would seem impossible that a man who was not himself a priest would ever be able to resist successfully the attempts of the ecclesiastical authorities to gain control of the various Communities—or even of the Society itself. Brother Henri was on the eve of receiving holy orders when his death occurred. The Superior considered this event to be a divine revelation: no Brother should ever be a priest—a rule that has always been faithfully observed.

To provide for the Brothers a retreat where they might occasionally rest from their labors, the Superior rented a place at Vaugirard, quite near Paris. In 1692, a regular novitiate was opened there with the approval of the Archbishop, who had recognized the Brothers as a religious community in the diocese. This House continued to serve its ' purpose until the year 1698, when, as the Institute counted more than sixty members, it no longer sufficed for the general retreats which it had become the custom to hold periodically. It was, therefore, decided to seek a larger house, for convenience in Paris and, if possible, in the parish of St. Sulpice. Such a place was found just beyond the Luxembourg gardens near the open country. It was an estate called "La Grand' Maison," for which the owner was willing to accept a very modest rental, as the house had the reputation of being haunted, and, consequently, it was difficult to obtain tenants for it. Thanks to the generosity of the parish priest of St. Sulpice and of a' lady, Mme des Voisins, the Superior was able to rent this property and transfer there the novitiate. It was here that the Brothers opened their first boarding school in 1698.

James II, the dethroned King of England, was at Saint-Germain-en-Laye, whither some loyal gentlemen had accompanied him into exile. Wishing to provide for the education of the sons of these gentlemen and also for that of some lads of loyalist Irish families, who had been sent to France for this purpose, King James consulted the Archbishop of Paris. His Grace advised the King to place these boys under the care of M. de la Salle. Though this school existed for only a short time—until this special group had finished its studies—it is of importance because it was the prototype of a kind of school with which the Brothers have been, and still are, so successful: a boarding school in which a well-balanced general education, particularly suited to the needs of the time and place, is provided for boys of the upper middle class.

It was about this time that the Brothers opened an entirely new sort of school: a Sunday school for young men whose work kept them busy on all other days of the week. This school must not be confused with the modern Sunday school for religious instruction alone; for, though such instruction was given, it did not dominate. The less advanced students were taught reading, writing, reckoning, and spelling, just as in the primary schools. The more advanced learned geometry, drawing, and architecture. It is to this school that Victor Duruy * made reference in his report on the project for technical instruction: "It is to the Abbé de la Salle that France is indebted for putting into practice and popularizing this instruction, which, if it had been regularly established, would have advanced by a century the organization of schools for adults and even of the specialized instruction of which our own epoch is so justly proud." †

Thanks to the numerous recruits to the Institute, the Brothers were able to comply with the requests of various bishops, who wished them to establish schools in their dioceses. Thus, the work of the Christian Schools entered upon a period of expansion. Two schools were opened in Chartres, and soon two more in Calais, one of which was for the sons of mariners. M. de la Salle sent Brother Gabriel Drolin to establish a school in Rome; there were, however, so many difficulties that the project was not realized until

* Minister of Public Instruction under the Second Empire.
† F. LAUDET, *op. cit.*, p. 82.

five years later. New schools were opened in Troyes and in Avignon, the latter soon becoming a center for the southern provinces.

Saint that he was, Jean-Baptiste de la Salle had his detractors. Great and holy though his work was, it had its critics. The Archbishop was influenced by them and informed M. de la Salle that he was no longer Superior of his Society; without a word of protest, the latter acquiesced. The Brothers, however, refused to agree; and when His Grace threatened their Founder with exile from Paris if he did not force them to obey, they boldly replied that they too would leave, which they at once began preparing to do. Thereupon, the parish priest of St. Sulpice hastened to the Archbishop, who recalled his threat of exile.

After many confabulations, held by the parish priest of St. Sulpice, M. de la Salle and the principal Brothers, it was agreed that, in order to appease the Archbishop, the Brothers would accept as nominal Superior the Abbé Bricot, whom he had appointed, provided the latter would promise to interfere with nothing and that he would visit them only once a month. The Abbé was so embarrassed by the part that he had been obliged to play that he withdrew shortly afterward. This was unfortunate, for he appears to have been a worthy man, which another priest who was appointed to succeed him does not seem to have been. This Superior sought in various ways to undermine the authority of the Founder, and he caused some defections among the Brothers. Finally, weary of petty persecution, M. de la Salle resolved to remit to the Archbishop the faculties which he held for hearing the confessions of the Brothers, thus resigning even the semblance of the contested office of Superior. His Grace, however, seems to have somehow changed his intentions, for he indicated that he wished M. de la Salle to continue to govern the Institute.

About this time a suit before the civil tribunal was brought against the Superior by the writing masters,* who accused the Brothers of infringing upon their privileges. M. de la Salle, convinced of the injustice of the charge, presented no defense. He was condemned by default, and a fine of fifty livres was imposed. All writing materials in their schools were to be seized, and the Brothers were ordered to instruct none but the children of the indigent and to teach them only such things as were suitable to their condition. The Brothers, acting upon instructions given them by their Superior, ignored the order and continued to teach as before. Further action was taken against them, and they were forbidden to live as a community until they had obtained royal letters patent. Some parish priests persisted in retaining the Brothers in their schools; but, in some cases, they were subject to so many vexations, such as confiscation of writing materials, books, and furnishings, as well as visits of inspection by the writing masters themselves to ascertain whether their pupils were really children of the poor, that they decided to give up these schools and disperse themselves among the new establishments of the Institute. To this the Superior agreed and assigned them

* Writing, as technical training, at least, was still taught by a separate group of teachers, either in their own schools or as visiting teachers. See Paul Monroe's *Cyclopedia of Education*, Vol. V, p. 420.

to divers schools in the provinces. But it was impossible to find suitable teachers in sufficient numbers to replace the Brothers; a compromise was effected: no child should be admitted to the parochial schools without a certificate of indigence.

V. Last Years of St. De la Salle

The troubles in Paris in no way interfered with the general progress of the Institute. A school was opened in Darnétal, near Rouen; and very soon afterward the Bureau of Charity of the city of Rouen decided to confide to the Brothers the direction of its schools. As in Paris, these schools drew some children from the pay schools, and the conflict began anew. The Bureau of Charity was forced to require certificates of indigence of all pupils who attended the schools of the Brothers. M. de la Salle submitted again, though such an arrangement was entirely at variance with his concept of the mission of the Institute: he wished that all children who presented themselves should be received into the schools, so that all relatively poor children might obtain a good and Christian education. In general, however, conditions were so satisfactory in Rouen that M. de la Salle formed the project of transferring the novitiate there from Paris. The Archbishop approved the idea and suggested that the domain of St. Yon, a property consisting of ample buildings surrounded by large grounds, be rented. It was here that the Brothers extended their work to three new fields of activity.

The nobility and the wealthy had their choice of many schools; the lower classes had access to numerous elementary schools—some pay, some free *—but the middle class, for which elementary instruction was not enough and a classical education a useless luxury, was in need of an advanced instruction in which the practical element would dominate. To satisfy this need, certain families of moderate means requested M. de la Salle to establish a boarding school in which their sons would be able to receive an education suitable to their social condition. This he agreed to do, giving thereby another proof of the breadth of mind with which he considered his mission and the flexibility with which he accommodated his system to the educational needs of the time and occasion.

The school was opened at St. Yon (about 1705), and it appears to be the first school in which the Brothers charged a regular tuition fee. In an old work on the city of Rouen, the program of studies is given as follows: "At St. Yon is taught everything pertaining to commerce, finance, military matters, architecture, mathematics: in short, all that a young man can learn except Latin." † In the *Dictionnaire de pédagogie,* we find the following admission: "Here is indeed, it must be admitted, the first beginning of higher primary instruction and the first plan of special secondary instruction." ‡ Another writer says: "The institution which grew from the boarding school at St. Yon is of historical interest, as exhibiting the germ of the French Higher Pri-

---

* A.-F. Villemain (Minister of Public Instruction), *Exposé des motifs et projets de la loi sur l'Instruction Secondaire, etc.,* p. 52, Paris, 1844. E. Allain, *loc. cit.*

† J. Guibert, *Vie de S. Jean-Baptiste de la Salle,* p. 182.

‡ F. Buisson, *op. cit.,* Part I, Tome I, p. 1110.

mary School of to-day and the German Latin-less *Real-schule*." *

A special division was created for students who had proved refractory to ordinary methods of education: each boy was placed in the care of a Brother who never lost sight of him. The studies of these "delinquents" were much the same as those of the other students, and they ate in the refectory with the latter. As their conduct improved, they were allowed more and more liberty.

The President of the Parliament of Normandy was so impressed by the success of the Brothers with these refractory lads that he determined to introduce a new procedure in the treatment of a certain class of juvenile offenders, who, he felt, would be contaminated by prison contacts, and he asked M. de la Salle to make the arrangements necessary to receive such subjects as might be sent to him by order of the Parliament or of the King's courts. After some hesitation, the Superior consented to establish at St. Yon what may be called a regular house of correction, and an isolated building was prepared for the prisoners. They were not subject to any harsh treatment. "The regulations resembled in no way those of a prison; rather were they like those of a boarding school where the limits of paternal discipline were not exceeded. To avoid wounding the susceptibilities of their families, the names of the inmates were kept secret, and their origins were known only to the Brother Director and the Prefect of Studies. These prisoners occupied themselves in various manners: they were allowed to grow flowers at their windows and keep birds

* J. W. ADAMSON, *Pioneers of Modern Education, 1600–1700*, p. 227, London, 1921.

in cages; some of them applied themselves to study and followed with the other students courses in geometry, drawing and architecture; others preferred manual work, and workshops were installed for their use, where they learned such things as cabinet-making and locksmithing." * This house of correction of the "Christian Brothers" existed already as early as 1710. The first general law decreeing the establishment of such institutions in Great Britain was passed in 1854. The state of Massachusetts had anticipated it by some six years.†

From the beginning, the Founder had made it a practice to visit regularly all the schools; but, as the number increased, he found it necessary to delegate a part of this duty, reserving for himself those in the North. He, however, set out to visit the schools in the South, as he wished to consider the possibility of establishing a novitiate there. In Avignon, he was again obliged to cope with difficulties created by the writing masters on the old charge that the Brothers were admitting to their schools children whose parents were able to pay for their instruction. However, the magistrates there were more liberal than those in the North: they did not require a certificate of indigence in order that a child might attend a charity school; they opened primary instruction to free competition. Such a decision was the beginning of free educational opportunity for all.

During a second visit to Avignon, a year later, the novitiate was established, and to its support both parish priests and laymen agreed to contribute. Many postulants pre-

* J. GUIBERT, *Histoire de S. Jean-Baptiste de la Salle,* p. 404.
† J. W. ADAMSON, *op. cit.,* p. 228.

sented themselves, and the outlook was most encouraging; but soon difficulties began to arise. Jansenism was at that time very active in the South. Jean-Baptiste de la Salle's devotion to his Catholic faith and his fidelity to the Holy See made it impossible for him to keep silent when attacks were made on them. From subsequent events, it would seem that much of the support given his work in the South was in reality due to a subtle plan by which it was hoped to win over to Jansenism a man of great influence and, at the same time, obtain the ascendancy over the schools of the Institute. As soon as the Superior had manifested his unswerving allegiance to the Church, everything changed: apparent friends became enemies, benefactors withdrew their aid, discord appeared among the novices and even to some extent among the Brothers.

Greatly discouraged, M. de la Salle went to Grenoble, where for about six months he replaced in the classroom the Brother Director, whom he sent to visit the schools in the North. The latter brought back a very unsatisfactory report: the Brother who was acting as Superior during M. de la Salle's absence had yielded to the demands of certain bishops to appoint priests as superiors of the Communities in their dioceses. The Brothers in Paris implored their Founder to return. He, however, contrary though it was to his wishes, was willing to let the arrangement be tested by time. Whereupon, the Brothers—who, being upon the spot, felt that they understood the urgency of the situation better than he did—wrote to their Founder, commanding him, with all respect, in the name of the obedience which he with them had promised the Institute, to return and take charge of its general government. Such a command could not be ignored, so he at once returned to Paris.

A year later, the novitiate—for which a new building had been erected—was moved from Paris to St. Yon, which now became in reality the Mother House. Once more established in Rouen, the Superior, besides taking an active interest in the novitiate, occupied himself with reforming the program of studies and the disciplinary regulations of the boarding school. Another matter of the greatest importance engaged his attention: his resignation as Superior and the election of his successor. The Brothers, warned by the increasing infirmities of their Founder, realized the necessity; it was, therefore, decided to send a Brother to visit the twenty-two Houses of the Society to obtain the consent of all the Brothers to the election of a Superior and the revision of the regulations. Five months later, this Brother returned with the necessary procurations.

Those Brothers who were able to be present were convoked for May 16, 1717, and the election took place three days later. In order that he might not be in a position to exert any special influence on the choice of his successor, the Superior refused to preside. Brother Barthélemy was elected. The Assembly then considered the revision of the regulations. After due deliberation, a few additions were made to the Rule which had been formulated in 1695 and which had been revised from time to time, as necessity arose. This text has been only slightly modified by subsequent general chapters; hence, the present Constitution of the Institute represents faithfully the spirit of the original Society.

M. de la Salle made one more visit to Paris, where, however, he did not stay with the Brothers. He feared lest his presence among them be embarrassing; for, though he was no longer Superior, yet their natural veneration for the Founder would prevent them from treating him as one of themselves. He stayed for a time with a community of priests, but this could not continue for long; it was not fitting that the Founder of the Institute should live—and perhaps die—away from his own Community, so Brother Barthélemy called him back to Rouen. With that spirit of order which had ever been present in his life and work, he at once set about arranging everything pertaining to the property of the Institute, so that his death would create for the Brothers no temporal difficulties. He also prepared for them a spiritual legacy in the form of a work entitled *Explication de la méthode d'oraison*.

St. Jean-Baptiste de la Salle died peacefully on Good Friday, April 17, 1719, surrounded by the Brothers of the Community and assisted by his parish priest. His body was interred in the parish church, whence it was removed in 1734 to the new chapel at St. Yon.

VI. The Institute since the Death of the Founder

Until the Revolution, the progress of the Institute was uninterrupted. The elementary schools increased in number, and the course of studies was improved. It was, however, in higher primary instruction that the greatest advance was made. There everything was to be created: new social conditions required changes in education, which the Brothers, being free from any traditional system, were particularly suited to develop. In several cities, boarding schools, like the one at St. Yon, were established. Schools were established abroad: at Estavayer in Switzerland, at Orvieto and Ferrara in Italy, and, though an unsuccessful attempt was made to found a school in Canada, a real college was opened in Martinique. At Boulogne, a commercial school was opened, in which special attention was given to writing, arithmetic, bookkeeping—single and double entry—and foreign exchange. An experiment was made with agricultural or horticultural studies at Cherbourg. At Montauban, the Brothers took charge of a free circulating library. Thus we find the Institute fostering various activities which were later to develop into great institutions.

In 1724, Louis XV granted the Institute letters patent for the jurisdiction of the Parliament of Rouen. The following year, Benedict XIII declared it a religious congregation officially recognized by the Church. Letters patent were later granted by Louis XVI for the jurisdictions of the Parliaments of Paris and Toulouse. The Brothers were empowered to train teachers, to keep free schools and boarding schools, and to receive delinquents sent to them by the courts.

Their ideal of free instruction did not meet with universal approval. The masters of the pay schools resented it, and certain liberals disapproved of their teaching the lower classes to read and write. La Chalotais says in his *Essay on National Education:* "The Brothers of the Christian Doctrine, who are called *Ignorantins,** have appeared to com-

* A popular name applied to the Brothers as teachers of the ignorant.

plete the ruin of everything. They teach reading and writing to people who ought to learn only to draw and to handle the plane and file." Voltaire wrote to him: "I thank you for forbidding laborers to study. I, who cultivate the earth, ask you for workmen and not for tonsured clerics. Above all, send me some Ignorantin Brothers to drive my plows or to yoke to them."

At the beginning of the Revolution it seemed that the Institute might be spared, so remote were the Brothers from all political activities, and so deservedly were they esteemed by the populace. However, when the decree of 1791 was issued, by which all persons engaged in public teaching were required to take an oath of submission to the civil constitution of the clergy, the Brothers could do nothing but abandon their schools, as such an oath could not be reconciled with their consciences. One year later, the Institute was suppressed on all French territory. In decreeing this suppression, the Assembly nevertheless declared that the Brothers had "deserved well of their country." *

In 1789, there were one hundred and twenty-one Communities of the Institute in France and six abroad—one thousand Brothers, with thirty-six thousand pupils in their schools.† It is difficult to estimate the true significance of these figures, as comparative statistics are scarce. We do know, however, that the total number of pupils enrolled in the secondary schools of the kingdom at that time was 72,747.‡ The Brothers then had in their schools—which were nearly all free—about half as many pupils as there were in

* J. Guibert, *Vie de S. Jean-Baptiste de la Salle*, p. 237.
† F. Laudet, *op. cit.*, p. 208.
‡ A.-F. Villemain, *op. cit.*, p. 55.

all the secondary schools in France. It may well be said that they had deserved well of their country.

During the Reign of Terror, some of the Brothers died on the scaffold or were drowned on the pontoons at Rochefort, others were deported, some enrolled in the army, a few continued their functions as private teachers, a very few made their way to the House in Rome. Only two Houses continued to exist: the one in Rome and the one in Orvieto.

When some degree of order had been reëstablished after the storm of revolution had passed, Napoleon decided to reorganize public instruction. On account of the scarcity of teachers, he was obliged to call upon the religious orders which had taught in the schools before the Revolution. The existence in France of the Brothers of the Christian Schools was legalized by decree in 1803. Immediately the surviving Brothers hastened to the House in Lyons, and Brother Frumence, who was Acting Superior with the title of Vicar General, came from Rome to assume the direction of the Society. The Brothers found a place in the educational system which Napoleon created and which is known as the Imperial University, a certain number of government schools having been entrusted to him. On the whole, the Imperial Government was interested chiefly in secondary and higher education. Primary instruction was for the most part left to the religious orders or to local initiative.

The Royal Government of the Restoration occupied itself to a much greater extent with primary instruction, and Louis XVIII was favorable to the Brothers. As a legally authorized congregation, their schools were subject only to the general supervision of the inspectors. Elementary education was to be based upon religion, respect for the law, and loyalty to the Sovereign. As this was entirely in accord with the principles of the Institute, the Brothers were able to devote themselves wholeheartedly to their work. In 1819, the Municipal Council of Paris offered the Brothers a house if they would move their Mother House and novitiate there. They accepted this offer in 1821.

The Revolution of 1830 did not, on the whole, adversely affect the Institute. Under Louis-Philippe, elementary instruction was organized, and it was required that there be a primary school in every commune. Although instruction was not entirely free, provision was made for children whose parents were unable to pay the small fees required. In each department was to be established a normal school. Both the communal schools and the normal schools could be entrusted to religious orders. Any citizen, provided he possessed a Certificate of Capacity, could teach the rudiments of learning. As a good many Brothers had their certificates, they availed themselves of the privilege accorded by the law.

The Second Empire was, in general, extremely well disposed toward the Brothers, and their work continued to expand. Brother Philippe, who was Superior from 1838 to 1874, established 1002 new Houses, of which 726 were in France and 276 abroad, the latter distributed as follows: 106 in Europe, 101 in the Americas, 43 in Africa, 26 in Asia.

Soon after it was definitely established, the Third Republic began to manifest the tendencies which were to characterize its policies more and more until the time of the World War.

In 1882 was enacted a law by which attendance at school became obligatory—this was excellent. Government schools were free to all—this was entirely in accord with the principle which the Institute had defended from its beginning. Religious instruction was prohibited in the schools—this was absolutely contrary to the concept of education held by the Brothers, and it made their position in the schools very difficult. However, since it was permitted them to give religious instruction, provided it was not in the schools or during school hours, they were able to reconcile their obligations as teachers in the schools of the Government with their duties as Christian educators.

In 1886, all members of religious orders were excluded by law from teaching in the Communal Schools; but they were still allowed to keep private schools, provided they complied with the necessary requirements in respect to certification, inspection, etc.

At the turn of the century, the Brothers had the satisfaction of witnessing the happy termination of the process of canonization of their venerated Founder. He had been declared Venerable in 1840; his beatification had been pronounced in 1888; and, on May 24, 1900, he was enrolled among the Saints of the Church by the Sovereign Pontiff Leo XIII.

In 1904, a law was passed which forbade any member of a religious order to teach in France. The Brothers were, therefore, obliged to abandon the great number of schools which Catholic charity had erected for them in all parts of the country. Thanks to the numerous establishments of the Institute abroad, it was in no danger of extinction, as at the time of the Revolution. The Mother House was transferred to Lembecq-les-Hal, a suburb of Brussels.

A delay of ten years was accorded the Institute in which

to terminate its legal existence in France. On August 1, 1914, the Secretary General of the Institute wrote to the Cardinal Archbishop of Paris: "The first day of September next marks the final limit of the legal existence of our Institute in France. Ministerial decrees order the closing of our last schools and even of our headquarters (*siège social*) in Paris." *

On this same August 1, 1914, the general mobilization was ordered; and by September 1, instead of the last of the Brothers leaving their mother country, hundreds, who had left long before, were returning to defend it. They were doing only their duty. One thousand nine hundred were mobilized; those who were too old to fight hastened to enroll in the sanitary service. Two hundred and eighty fell on the field of battle.

There are today over 1200 Houses of the Brothers: in Europe, Asia, Africa, Australia, the two Americas, and the islands of the seas. There are 14,911 Brothers, and in the schools 313,436 pupils. Of these pupils 166,758 are in free schools. In addition to this number of Community Brothers, there are 6148 aspirants to the order: juniors, novices, and scholastics.

VII. The Pedagogy of St. De la Salle

From the beginning of the Christian Schools, St. De la Salle worked to establish uniformity among the teachers; and to this end he wrote for them instructions from time to time. Already, by 1690, the general principles of his method were established, and about 1695 he united his writings in a didactic work, which he entitled *Conduite des écoles*. The future teachers all made copies of this work,

* F. Laudet, *op. cit.*, p. 220.

which they studied during their training; but not until
was a printed edition published.* In subsequent year.,
printed version was often revised to meet the changing needs
of time—and even of place.† However, we are concerned
only with the edition of 1720, which, since we are told that
all changes in it were approved by him, undoubtedly represents the ideas of the Founder.‡

The aim of the early Christian Schools is clearly indicated.
It was essentially toward making good Catholics—good
Christians—of the children of the poorer classes. "It is for
this reason that the schools are kept," says the Rule, "so
that the children being under their direction from morning
until evening, the teachers may teach them how to live
well, by instructing them with Christian maxims, and by
giving them the education which is suited to them. . . . It
is with the view of procuring these advantages for the children of artisans and of the poor that the Christian Schools
have been instituted." § This aim was so important in the
eyes of the Founder that he devoted a great part of the
time spent in school to religious exercises and to instruction
in Christian Doctrine. This insistence upon the religious element in the education and life of the pupils may appear
excessive to some people; but when we consider the definite
objective of the Brothers and the fact that theirs were schools
taught by devoted and devout Catholics for the voluntary
and free use of exclusively Catholic children, we must admit

* J. GUIBERT, *Histoire de S. Jean-Baptiste de la Salle,* p. 200.
† There is a greatly modified evolution of the work, adapted
for use of schools in America, called *Management of Christian
Schools.*
‡ See p. 46.
§ J. GUIBERT, *op. cit.,* p. 203.

that the emphasis placed upon religious training is quite in place.

The number of prayers taught the individual pupil is certainly not excessive: just those that he would need for his daily private devotions and in order to take part in most public devotions. These prayers were taught in both Latin and French: in Latin, for the purpose of participating in the offices of the Church; in French, so that they might be fully understood. Great care was to be taken to render the religious instruction effective. "The teacher will not speak to his pupils as though he were preaching, but he will question them continuously. . . . He will make use in his questions only of simple expressions and of words that are easy to understand. . . . He will never fail, in every Catechism lesson, to make some practical application." *

A practical method was devised to teach the children the duty of almsgiving as well as to help the poorest among them. "A small basket will be placed in each classroom, into which the children may put what bread they have left over, when they are so piously inclined, to be distributed among those who are poor." As a check on unjustified generosity, "the teacher will see that they do not give away any of their bread unless they have enough left for themselves." † Surely a very simple and direct method of inculcating the Catholic principle of charity, that out of our abundance we must give to the poor, and of practicing the first of the Corporal Works of Mercy: Feed the hungry. At the present time, such a method would doubtless be considered humiliating to the recipients and conducive to self-righteousness on the part

* See pp. 129 ff.
† See p. 55.

of the bestowers. For the good people of the seventeenth century, however, poverty was no disgrace: it was just the will of God, to be borne like any other misfortune; and charity within one's means was just one of the precepts of the Church, to be obeyed without self-gratulation.

One must use a great deal of reserve in judging matters pertaining to another epoch from the point of view of the present: *Autres temps, autres mœurs.* This is a thought that it would be well to bear in mind when we come to the question of corporal punishments.

It has been asserted that the early Brothers were very harsh in their punishments. In comparison with school usages of today—those of the Brothers as well as others—this may in a manner be true. In those days, such punishments were the rule. Louis XIII and Louis XIV were thrashed in their youth, and so were schoolboys in general, everywhere and for a long time afterward. St. De la Salle urged the greatest care in inflicting punishments. They were to be rare, and only when all other means of correction had failed was recourse to be had to corporal punishment, which was to be administered with all circumspection.

That a child should be expected to kneel and thank his teacher for having punished him may well cause the modern minded—for whom punishment is something that is avoided if one is clever enough or grudgingly accepted otherwise—to smile or to protest that hypocrisy was being inculcated. A little consideration of the religious philosophy that then prevailed ought, however, to show the matter in a very different light. Disobedience to proper authority was considered a very serious fault, for which the offender should feel sincere contrition and willingly accept penance. Hence, to have been brought to contrition, to have received the penance and expiated the fault would be in truth a cause for gratitude to be publicly and willingly expressed.

Though bad conduct was to be punished only when punishment was unavoidable, good conduct was to be rewarded whenever reward was possible. The highest rewards were for piety, as piety was attainable by all and of the greatest importance in education. Thus, we find in the *Conduite des écoles* a system of punishments and rewards, established, it is true, in conformity with the usages of a time when it was deemed that to spare the rod, when necessary, was indeed to spoil the child, but with a decided tendency toward benevolence.

In the interest of order and discipline, the employment of the entire day was regulated down to the least detail. Orderly conduct on the way to and from school was required. Silence in the classroom was enjoined—and well it may have been, for each Brother might in those early days have in his class from sixty to a hundred pupils.* So that even the teachers might speak as little as possible, a code of signals was devised. To facilitate the general management of such large classes, various class officers were appointed.

The manner of recitation was what is known as the simultaneous method: all the pupils of the same class recited at the same time, one after another; and those who were not reciting were required to follow attentively. Though a commonplace in our time, this was quite an innovation

---

* In 1691, in the school in the rue Princesse, there were 300 pupils divided into four classes with three teachers; in that of the rue du Bac, there were 120 pupils with two teachers. J. Guibert, *op. cit.*, p. 199.

then: the general usage was to have each pupil recite while the others studied—or played. The more adv students were required to aid the others in preparing t. tasks.

The program of studies comprised religious instruction, reading, spelling, grammar, arithmetic, the system of weights and measures, and deportment: the children were expected to bring their morning meal to school so that they might learn to eat properly. This is a thoroughly practical and fairly complete elementary course, which well deserves the following commendation: "The course of study prescribed for the schools of the Institute by the *Conduct* is one which under any circumstances would make a by no means un-satisfactory elementary program. It deserves much more than this lukewarm praise when one remembers that the school-life of the pupils was brief, and that Europe was only just awakening to the need for popular education.*

The reading of Latin—that is, to pronounce the words— was taught, but only after the reading of French had been mastered. This was a decided innovation: in all the ele-mentary schools in France in the seventeenth century, the pupils were taught to read Latin first. The reason given for this procedure is that, French being more difficult to spell and pronounce, one should begin with the easier of the two. For children who needed to learn Latin in order to pursue higher studies later, there is much truth in this theory; but for those who would never go beyond the ele-mentary schools and would perhaps remain only two years or so in school, good sense dictated that they should be taught reading by means of the mother tongue.

* J. W. Adamson, *op. cit.*, p. 234.

To raise the question whether St. De la Salle was inspired by the example of the Port-Royalists or of the Oratorians, who also taught French first, would be beside the point. For him, it was merely whether children should be taught to read by means of Latin or of French words and not at all a question of the language in which instruction should be given, as it was in the former cases.

Every branch of study is regulated in the *Conduite des écoles,* and it may well be said that "modern pedagogy could, in spite of the progress in this domain, profit by many of these details." *

Throughout the treatise, the aim of the instruction in the Christian Schools is ever apparent: to make of poor children good Catholic Christians, well instructed in their religious duties and practices; to render them capable of earning their living in that state of life in which they have been placed or even able, thanks to the practical instruction which they have received, to rise to a somewhat higher station.

The means by which these objectives are to be attained are quite as constantly and clearly indicated: sound religious instruction, frequent prayer, practical precept, and good example; careful instruction in a limited but thoroughly practical and suitable course of study; absolute attention to detail; accurate and faithful performance of duties.

Rewards and punishments should be used to help obtain the desired results: if a child works well, he should be rewarded; if he is lazy or obstinate, recourse should be had to punishment; punishment should be sparing, it should be

* JULES HERMENT, *Les idées pédagogiques de Saint Jean-Baptiste de la Salle,* p. 73.

proportionate to the offense, it should be remedial, it should be administered in charity and received in humility.

In such few words can be summed up the simple pedagogic and moral principles that permeate the *Conduite des écoles* and constitute the substance of the educational philosophy of St. De la Salle.

THE CONDUCT

OF

THE CHRISTIAN SCHOOLS

DIVIDED INTO TWO PARTS

Attend to thyself and to doctrine; be earnest in them; for in doing this thou shalt both save thyself and them that hear thee. (I Epistle to Timothy, 4, 16.)

AT AVIGNON

By Joseph Charles Chastanier, Printer and Book-seller, near the College of the Reverend Jesuit Fathers.

M.D.CC.XX.

WITH PERMISSION OF THE SUPERIORS

LETTER

AD MAJOREM
DEI GLORIAM

To the Brothers of the Christian Schools.

My very dear Brothers:

The ardent zeal which you have hitherto manifested in the exercise of the ministry with which God has honored you impels me to exhort you to continue to perfect yourselves in an occupation so holy and useful to the Church as yours. There is nothing greater than to dedicate oneself to giving to children a Christian education and to inspiring them with the fear and love of God: it is for this purpose that you have consecrated yourselves to His service—a blessed consecration which will increase your reward in the Kingdom of Heaven, according to the promise of Our Lord Jesus Christ.

This is what our venerable Founder never ceased to bring to your attention during his lifetime. Ah! what did he not do to this end? With what care and solicitude did he seek to provide you with the means of fulfilling your duties with as much prudence as charity? You can bear witness, and God knows it, with what attention and what charity he sought, together with the principal and most experienced Brothers of the Institute, suitable means of maintaining among you a holy uniformity in your manner of educating

45

youths. He drew up in writing all that he believed to be expedient for that purpose, and he prepared a Method of Conducting Schools, which he exhorted you to read again and again, in order to learn from it what would be most useful to you. Your conformity with his desire and the care which you still take to put into practice what he taught you show clearly enough your zeal and your veneration of so worthy a father.

This Method of Conducting Schools, my dear Brothers, was soon introduced into all the Houses of the Institute, where everyone gloried in conforming to it. However, as there were several things in it that could not be put into practice, the Brothers of the Assembly which was held for the purpose of electing the first Brother Superior represented to M. de la Salle that it would be expedient to make some corrections. He approved their proposition, and thus it was put into better order than it had been before.

You indicated clearly, my dear Brothers, by the eagerness with which you requested that the work thus corrected should be sent to all your Houses, the extent of your approval of what the Brothers of this Assembly had done; and the repeated demands which you still make for copies of this work prove sufficiently your desire for uniformity of method. But lack of leisure has always prevented the preparation of a sufficient number of copies to satisfy your just desires; and, furthermore, there frequently appear a number of errors, due to lack of accuracy on the part of the copyists, which often change the sense.

At length, some of the most zealous Brothers, sympathizing with the difficulty which you experience in being thus deprived of something so necessary, have entreated our very honored Brother Superior to allow the work to be printed. He has consented, all the more willingly because he himself has for a long time desired to afford you this satisfaction. He has read it again with great attention and had it carefully examined in order to eliminate all that might be useless.

Accept, then, my very dear Brothers, the offer which I make you of a book which already belongs to you by so many rights. Seek therein the prudence and wisdom that are so necessary for you to establish the reign of God in the souls which are confided to you, and be sure that if you persevere in so holy a work you will save your own souls, and you will save many others as well. Amen.

(Brother Barthélemy, 1720)

PREFACE

It has been necessary to prepare this Method of Conducting Christian Schools so that all may be uniform in these schools and in all the places where there are Brothers of this Institute and that the usages may always be the same. Man is so subject to laxity, and even to change, that he must have written rules to keep him within the limits of his duty and to prevent him from introducing something new or from destroying what has been wisely established. This method has been prepared and put in order (by the late M. de la Salle) only after a great number of conferences between him and the oldest and most capable teachers among the Brothers of the Institute, and after several years of experience. Nothing has been added that has not been thoroughly deliberated and well tested, and of which the advantages and disadvantages have not been weighed and, in so far as possible, the good or bad consequences have not been foreseen. The Brothers will, therefore, take great care to observe all that is therein prescribed, being persuaded that there will be order in the schools only to the extent that they are careful to omit nothing; and they will receive this Method of Conducting Schools as though it were given them by God through the instrumentality of their Superiors and the first Brothers of the Institute.

This book is divided into three parts. The first part treats of all the exercises and everything else that is done in school from the opening until the closing hour. The second sets forth the necessary and useful means of which the teachers should avail thmselves in order to bring about and maintain order in the schools. The third part treats, firstly, of the duties of the Inspector of Schools; secondly, of the care and diligence to be observed by the trainer of new teachers; thirdly, of the qualities which the teachers should have or should acquire, of the conduct which they should maintain in order to acquit themselves well of their duties in the schools; and, fourthly, of these things to be observed by the students. The third part will be only for the use of the Brothers Directors and those who are charged with the training of new teachers.*

The Brothers Directors of the Houses of the Institute and the Inspectors of Schools will apply themselves to learning well and to knowing perfectly all that is contained in this book and will proceed in such a manner that the teachers will observe exactly all the practices that are prescribed for them—even the least—in order to procure by this means great order in the schools, a well-regulated and uniform conduct on the part of the teachers who will be in charge of them, and a very considerable result for the children who will be taught. The teachers in the schools will read and read again often in it what is suitable for them, so that they may be ignorant of nothing and may become faithful to it in their practices.

* This third part is not contained in the copy from which this translation was made. As stated above, it was for the use only of Directors and trainers of teachers.

THE CONDUCT OF THE CHRISTIAN SCHOOLS

FIRST PART

SCHOOL EXERCISES AND THE MANNER OF CONDUCTING THEM

CHAPTER I

ENTERING AND BEGINNING SCHOOL

ARTICLE I

ENTRANCE OF PUPILS

THE doors of the schools will be opened at all times at half past seven o'clock in the morning and at one o'clock in the afternoon. In the morning as well as in the afternoon, the pupils will always have half an hour in which to assemble.

Care will be taken that they do not assemble in a crowd in the street before the door is opened and that they do not make noises by crying out or singing.

They will not be permitted to amuse themselves by playing and running in the vicinity of the school during this time or to disturb the neighbors in any manner whatsoever; but care will be taken that they walk so properly in the street in which the school is situated and that they remain afterward before the door, while waiting for it to open, in such good order that those who pass will be edified. The

Head Teacher or Inspector of Schools will assign one of the most reliable pupils to observe those who make noises while assembling. This pupil will merely observe without commenting at the time and will afterward tell the teacher what has happened, without the others' being aware of it.

When the door is opened, care will be taken that the pupils do not rush forward and enter in a crowd but that they enter in an orderly fashion, one after another.

The teachers will be attentive and take care that all the pupils walk so lightly and so sedately while entering the school that their steps will not be heard, that they remove their hats before taking holy water, that they make the sign of the cross, and that they go at once directly to their classroom.

It will be instilled into them that they must enter the classroom with profound respect, out of consideration for the presence of God. When they have reached the center of the room, they will make a low bow before the crucifix and will salute the teacher if he is present. Then they will kneel to adore God and to say a short prayer to the Blessed Virgin, after which they will arise, again bow before the crucifix in the same manner, salute the teacher, and go sedately and silently to their regular places.

While the pupils are assembling and entering the classroom, they will all maintain such complete silence that not the least noise will be heard—not even of the feet—so that it will not be possible to distinguish those who are entering, nor to notice that the others are studying.

Having reached their seats, they will remain quietly in them, without leaving them for any reason whatsoever until the teacher enters.

The teachers will take care to give warning that those who have talked or made any noise in the classroom during their absence will be punished and that they will not forgive offenses against silence or good order committed during this time.

From the time of entering the school until the arrival of the teacher, those of the pupils who know how to read will study the Catechism, but so quietly that they cannot be heard by the others and that not even any noise may be heard in the classroom.

During this time, there will be a pupil in the first class who will be charged by the teacher to point out on the two charts—of the alphabet and of the syllables—first one letter or syllable and then another in different places, so that the pupils who are learning them may thus study their lessons. Those who are studying all the lessons of each chart will read one after another in the order in which they are seated. While the one who is reading is saying aloud a letter or syllable, all the others will observe it on the chart, and each of them will say it in a tone so low that he will be heard only by the two who are next to him. The pupil who has been chosen to point out the contents of the charts will do so without correcting and without saying a single word: the teacher will take care above all that he be faithful in this.

The teachers will be most careful that all the pupils be in the classroom before their own arrival and that none should come late, except rarely, for good reasons and through necessity. They will be very exact in requiring that this point be observed, and the Inspector of Schools will pay special attention to it, even warning the parents when receiving pupils that they must come every day at the exact hour and that he will receive them only on this condition.

ENTRANCE OF TEACHERS AND BEGINNING OF SCHOOL

The teachers will go to the classrooms as soon as the Rosary has been said in the morning; likewise in the afternoon, at once after the litany of Saint Joseph, without stopping anywhere.

They will walk with great decorum and in silence, not rapidly, but sedately, with great reserve of demeanor and glance.

On entering the school they will uncover, take holy water, bow before the crucifix, make the sign of the cross. After having said a short prayer and again bowed before the crucifix, they will go to their accustomed places.

When the teachers enter the school, all the pupils of each class will rise and remain standing until their teacher has reached his place; those before whom he passes will salute him when he kneels to say his prayer, and none will sit down until he is seated.

If the Brother Director or any strangers visit the school, the pupils will conduct themselves in the same manner only the first time they enter; and in case they remain and go from one class to another, the pupils will remain uncovered until the teacher makes them a sign to be seated and to put on their hats.

From the time the teachers take their seats until school begins, they will apply themselves to reading the New Testament and will remain silent in order to give an example to the pupils, observing, however, all that takes place in the school, so as to maintain good order.

School will always begin punctually at eight o'clock in the morning and at half past one in the afternoon. At the last stroke of eight o'clock and the last stroke of half past one o'clock, a pupil will ring the bell of the school, and at the first sound of the bell all the pupils will kneel, with their arms crossed and their eyes lowered, in a very modest posture and manner.

As soon as the bell has ceased ringing, the Reciter of Prayers will begin the prayers aloud in a raised voice, distinctly and sedately, and after making the sign of the cross, all the pupils making it with him, he will begin the *Veni Sancte Spiritus,* which the other pupils will continue to say with him but in a lower tone. They will, in the same manner, say with him the rest of the prayers prescribed in the Manual of Prayers of the Christian Schools. In the morning, the Reciter of Prayers will say the blessing before the meal in Latin, *Benedicite,* and after breakfast the Act of Thanksgiving, *Agimus tibi Gratias, etc.;* whereas in the afternoon they will be said in French, as is indicated in the Manual of Prayers.

When the prayers are finished, the teachers will clap their hands, and the pupils will rise and breakfast in silence.

CHAPTER II

Breakfast and Lunch

ARTICLE I

Things to Which the Teachers Must Attend during Breakfast and Lunch

The teachers should take care that the pupils bring with them every day their breakfast and lunch, and, without obliging them to do so, a little basket will be placed in an appointed place in the classroom, into which the children, when they are so piously inclined, may put what bread they have left over to be distributed among those of them who are poor. The teacher will see that they do not give away any of their bread unless they have enough left for themselves. Those who have bread to give will raise their hands, showing at the same time the piece of bread which they have to give, and a pupil who has been appointed to receive these alms will go to get them. At the end of the meal, the teachers will distribute the bread to the poorest and will exhort them to pray to God for their benefactors.

The teachers will also take care that the pupils do not throw either nuts or shells on the floor: he will oblige them to put them into their pockets or into their bags.

They must be made to understand that it is desired that they eat in school in order to teach them to eat with propriety, with decorum, and in a polite manner and to invoke God before and after eating.

The teachers will see that the pupils do not play during breakfast and lunch but that they be very attentive to the exercises that are being done in school during this time; and in order to discover whether they are exact in the performance of this duty, they will, from time to time, make one of them repeat what has been said, excepting those who are occupied in writing.

The pupils will not be permitted to give anything whatsoever one to another—not even any part of their breakfast —nor to exchange it.

The teachers will see, in so far as possible, that the pupils finish breakfast by half past eight o'clock.

ARTICLE II

WHAT IS DONE DURING BREAKFAST AND LUNCH

On the first two days of the week upon which school is held all day, the pupils who read but do not spell will repeat the morning prayers during breakfast and the evening prayers during lunch. For those who are in the writing classes, on Mondays and Tuesdays, there will be one pupil who will occupy an appointed place and who will say in an audible tone all the prayers: during breakfast, the morning prayers; in the afternoon, the evening ones, the Commandments of God, those of the Church, and the *Confiteor*. The pupils will take turns in doing this. They will be obliged to learn these prayers by heart and will repeat them during breakfast and lunch on these days. The Inspector will reprove them when they fail. On the last two days of the week upon which school is held throughout the whole day, they will repeat during breakfast and lunch what they have learned of the Diocesan Catechism during the week. The teacher will see that they all, without a single exception, recite on these two days. What is to be learned in each class in a week will be indicated by the Brother Director or the Head Teacher.

On Wednesdays, when there is a whole holiday on Thursday, or on those days upon which there is a half holiday, if there is a holy day of obligation during the week, those who read Latin will repeat the responses of Holy Mass during breakfast, and likewise during the first half hour of the Catechism in the afternoon.

If there are in the class in which the responses of Holy Mass are recited any pupils who already know them or are capable of learning them, even though they are not yet able to read Latin, the teacher will take care that they know them well and will make them repeat them also.

The pupils who recite all the above-mentioned things should have learned them by heart at home or during the time that they are assembling in school. It will not be in order to learn them that they repeat them, but only to show that they know them; and, in respect to the prayers and responses of Holy Mass, to learn how to say them properly. Those who do not know them, although they have already been a long time in the writing class, will also be made to learn and to recite them.

All the pupils who recite the prayers and responses of Holy Mass will repeat them, each in turn and one after the other in succession, in a section separate from the one reciting the other prayers.

In the lower classes, the prayers will be repeated in the following manner: One of two pupils will recite the titles of the prayers, and the other will recite the Acts or the Articles, all in order and in succession from the beginning of the prayers to the end. Each of them will do both of these things in turn.

The one who recites the titles of the prayers and the questions of the Catechism will correct the other in case he fails in anything, and in case he does not do this the teacher will take care to make a sign to him. If the pupil does not know what has been said incorrectly, the teacher whose duty it is at the time to attend both to those who are reciting and to the order of the whole class will make a sign to another pupil to correct him in the same manner as in the lessons.

In the writing class, as the teacher will be occupied in writing, a pupil who has been appointed Inspector will do what the teacher should do, but in respect to this recitation only, for the teacher should in no way exempt himself from watching over the general order of the class during this time.

The responses of Holy Mass will be recited in the following manner: Throughout the whole recitation, one pupil will do what the priest should do and will say what he should say, as is indicated in the liturgy. Another pupil, who will be at his side, will reply what the server should reply and do what he should do.

The server will do accurately all that is indicated in the Manual of Prayers of the Christian Schools. Those who are reciting the prayers and responses of Holy Mass will maintain throughout this time a very decorous and pious attitude. They should hold their hands properly, and their demeanor should be most respectful. They should be obliged to recite these prayers and responses with the same piety and the same respect, with the same demeanor and in the same manner that would be desirable if they were serving Holy Mass or saying their prayers at home.

The teacher will take care that those who are reciting the prayers and the responses of Holy Mass or the Catechism should, during this time, speak very distinctly and in a moderately loud tone, so that all may hear them. Nevertheless, they should speak low enough to oblige the other pupils to keep silent, to listen, and to be attentive to those who are reciting.

During this time, the teacher will observe very carefully everything that happens in the class, and he will make sure that all are attentive. From time to time, he will stop those who are reciting in order to question those who he notices are not sufficiently attentive to what has been said; and if the latter are unable to answer, he will impose some penance upon them or will punish them, as he may judge necessary.

During this recitation, the teacher will hold either the Manual of Prayers or the Catechism, and he will take care that the pupils repeat very exactly and very well.

On the first two days of the week and the two days upon which the Catechism is to be recited, those who are learning their letters from the alphabet chart will learn and repeat only the *Pater Noster,* the *Ave Maria,* the *Credo,* and the *Confiteor* in Latin and in French, as they are in the Manual of Prayers of the Christian Schools.

Those who are learning from the chart of syllables will learn and repeat the Acts of Entering the Presence of God, of Invocation of the Holy Ghost, of Adoration and of Thanksgiving, which come in sequence at the beginning of the morning prayers as well as of the evening prayers.

Those who are spelling from the primer will learn and repeat consecutively, in the following order, the Offering and Petition, which are in the morning prayers; the Act of Presenting Ourselves to God, the Confession of Sins, the Acts of Contrition and of Offering of Sleep, which are in the evening prayers; the prayer to the Guardian Angel and those which follow in the morning prayers as well as in the evening prayers.

If any who are studying the last two of these three lessons do not know any of the prayers that should have been learned in the lesson or in the preceding ones, the teacher will make them learn and repeat these prayers with those pupils who are studying the lesson in which such prayers should be learned—for instance, with those who are studying the alphabet, if they do not know the *Pater Noster,* the *Ave Maria,* the *Credo,* and the *Confiteor.* But when they know them well, or supposing they know them well, they will learn with those who are reading from the chart of syllables the Acts that should be repeated by the pupils who are studying this lesson.

Those who are spelling or reading in the second book will learn and repeat all the prayers, the morning prayers as well as the evening prayers. If the teacher observes that anyone who is reciting these prayers does not know them well, he will oblige him to learn them privately from the Manual of Prayers of the Christian Schools, and he will fix a time for him to repeat them, either entirely or in part, as he will see fit.

If there are in the same class any pupils who should recite the Catechism, they will do so only on Saturday or on the last school day of the week, and if during breakfast and lunch on this day there is more time than is needed to have all of them recite it, the time that remains will be employed in having the prayers recited.

On the days of the week on which the others are reciting the responses of Holy Mass, the latter will learn to say the Rosary and will repeat it, two together, in the following manner:

They will stand facing each other and will both make simultaneously the sign of the cross, after which one of them will say the versicle *Dignare me laudare te Virgo Sacrata* and the response, *Da mihi virtutem contra hostes tuos.*

Then, the first one will say on the cross *Credo in unum Deum, etc.* On the large bead which comes immediately after, he will say the *Pater Noster,* and, on each of the three little beads which follow, he will say an *Ave Maria,* at the end of which he will say *Gloria Patri, etc.* and *sicut erat in principio, etc.* He will continue in the same manner to say the decade that follows, and when it is completed he will again say the *Gloria Patri, etc.* When he has finished, the other will repeat aloud and intelligibly all that his companion has just recited. They will say thus, one after the other, only this decade, and the teacher will make them understand that in order to say the chaplet they must say six decades,* just as they have said this one.

They will be made to say after this decade *Maria, Mater*

---

* To the five decades which constitute a third part of the Rosary and form a chaplet the Brothers of the Christian Schools add a sixth decade in honor of the Immaculate Conception, which is said for the special intention of the Order.

gratiæ, Mater misericordiæ, tu nos ab hostes protege et in hora mortis suscipe; and they will be taught that this is to be said at the end of the chaplet.

Those who do not know how to say the Rosary will be taught to say it in this manner.

When reciting the prayers, all the pupils who are studying these four different kinds of lessons will be in the same section, and they will all repeat, one after another, the prayers that they are to learn, beginning with those who are learning the alphabet and ending with those who are spelling and reading in the second book.

CHAPTER III

STUDIES

ARTICLE I

THE COURSE OF STUDIES

Section I

General Observations on the Course of Studies

There will be nine different grades of instruction in the Christian Schools: First, the table of the alphabet. Second, the table of syllables. Third, the primer. Fourth, the second book for learning to spell and read by syllables. Fifth, the same second book, in which those who know how to spell perfectly will begin to read. Sixth, the third book which will be used to teach to read with pauses. Seventh, the Psalter.

Eighth, the book on Christian Civility.* Ninth, letters written by hand.

All the students of all these grades, with the exception of those who are reading the alphabet and the syllables, will be distributed in three sections: the first composed of the beginners, the second of the intermediate, and the third of the advanced and of those who are perfect in the work of the grade.

The beginners are not called thus because they are only beginning the grade; for a number of them might remain a long time in this section because they did not advance sufficiently to be placed in a higher one.

The beginners' section for each grade will then be composed of those who still make many mistakes in reading the lesson. The intermediate section will consist of those who make few mistakes in this reading, that is to say, one or two mistakes at most each time. In the section of the advanced and perfect will be those who ordinarily make no mistakes in reading their lessons.

There will, however, be only two sections of readers of the book on Christian Civility. The first section will be composed of those who make mistakes in reading it, and the second of those who make almost none.

Each of these sections for the various grades will have its assigned place in the school, so that the pupils of one section will not be mixed with those of another section of the same grade—for instance, the beginners with the intermediate—but may be easily distinguished the ones from the others by means of their places.

*J. B. DE LA SALLE, *Règles de la bienséance et de la civilité chrétienne,* written in 1695.

All the students of a same grade will, however, follow the lessons together without distinction or discrimination, as the teacher will require of them.

It is not possible in this Method of Conducting Schools to limit the duration of the lessons of each class, because the number of pupils in each grade is not always the same; and for this reason it will be the duty of the Brother Director or of the Inspector of Schools to prescribe the time allotted to each lesson in each class.

All the students of each grade will have the same book and will have their lessons together. The least advanced will always be made to read first, beginning with the simplest lesson and ending with the most difficult one.

In the highest class, in the afternoon, however, when there are some pupils who are not writing, those who write will be made to read first, and the others will read after the writers have read, even during the time for writing, until half past three o'clock.

Section II

The Posture Which the Teachers and Pupils Should Maintain and the Manner in Which They Should Deport Themselves during Lessons

The teachers should always be seated, or they should stand in front of their seats during all lessons—those on the alphabet and syllables as well as those in books or letters written by hand.

They should not leave their places except in cases of grave necessity, and they will find such necessity very rare if they take a little care.

They will be careful to maintain a very modest demeanor and to deport themselves with great seriousness, never allowing themselves to descend to anything base or to behave like a child or pupil, such as to laugh or to do anything that might excite the pupils.

This seriousness which is demanded of the teachers does not consist in having a severe or austere aspect, in getting angry or in saying harsh words; but it consists in a great reserve in their gestures, in their actions, and in their words.

The teachers will above all be cautious not to become familiar with the pupils, not to speak to them in a careless manner, and not to suffer the pupils to speak to them other than with great respect.

A teacher, in order that he may acquit himself well of his duty, must be trained to do the following three things: First, he must watch over all the pupils so that he may incite them to do their duty, may keep them in order and maintain silence. Second, he must keep in hand during all the lessons the book which is at that time being read, and he must follow the reader exactly. Third, he must pay attention to the one who is reading and to the manner in which he reads, so that he may correct him when he fails.

The pupils should always be seated during the lessons, even while reading from the charts of the alphabet and the syllables; and they should hold their bodies erect and keep their feet on the floor in good order. Those who are reading the alphabet and the syllables should have their arms crossed, and those who are reading in books should hold their books in both hands, resting them neither upon their knees nor upon the table. They should also look straight before them, their faces turned slightly in the direction of the teacher, who must take care that they do not turn their heads so much that they may be able to speak with their companions and that they do not turn first to one side and then to the other.

While one of the pupils is reading, all the others who are having the same lesson will follow in their books, which they should always have in their hands.

The teacher will take great care to see that all read to themselves what the reader is reading aloud, and from time to time he will make some of them read a few words in passing, so as to surprise them and find out if they are following effectively. If they are not following, the teacher will impose upon them some penance or punishment; and if he notices that some of them do not like to follow or more easily or more frequently neglect to do so, he will be careful to make them read last, and even several different times, a little each time, so that the others may also have the time to read. All who are studying the same lesson will remove their hats at the beginning of the lesson, and they will not replace them until they have read.

If the teacher makes them read several times, the second, the third, and the other times they will take off their hats when they begin to read, and they will replace them as soon as they have finished.

Section III

How the Teachers Should Prepare the Pupils for Promotion

The teachers will not promote, either from any grade or from any section, any pupils in their classes; they will merely present to the Brother Director or the Inspector of Schools those whom they believe to be fit for promotion.

The teachers will be particularly careful not to present for promotion any pupil who is not very capable. Pupils easily become discouraged when they have been recommended by the teacher and are not promoted by the Brother Director or the Inspector.

In order that no teacher may be mistaken in regard to the fitness of his pupils for promotion, all the teachers will examine, toward the end of each month, on a day fixed by the Brother Director or the Inspector of Schools, those pupils in all grades and in all sections who should be ready for promotion at the end of that month.

After this examination, the teachers will mark on their class lists, by a pin mark before each name, those whom they consider capable of being promoted; and if there are any whose capacity may seem to them doubtful or may not appear to them to be sufficient for promotion to a more advanced grade or to a higher section of the same grade, they will mark them in the same place by two pin marks, so that the Brother Director may examine them more carefully. In regard to the writers, the teacher will mark on the class lists those whom he judges capable of being promoted in writing, by marking them on the left close to the name; and those whom he judges capable of being promoted to a higher section in writing or in reading manuscripts he will also mark, on the right close to the name. Those whom he judges capable of being promoted in arithmetic, he will mark farther away, close to the line on the left of the column in which are marked those who were tardy.

For promotions in the Christian Civility or in reading

manuscripts, a pinprick will be placed after the surname of the pupil; and for promotions in arithmetic a mark will be placed farther away, before the column used to mark the late-comers. Doubtful cases will be indicated by two pinpricks.

The teachers will agree with the Brother Director upon those who might be promoted, but whom it would not be opportune to promote at the time: either because they are too young or because it is necessary to leave some in each grade or each section who know how to read well enough to stimulate the others and serve them as models; to train them to express themselves well, to pronounce distinctly the letters, syllables, and words, and to make the pauses well.

The teachers will take care, some time before the day upon which the promotions are to be made, to inform those pupils whom the Brother Director or the Inspector has agreed not to promote—either for their own good, because they are too young, or for the good of the class and the grade, in order that there be some who can support the others. They will do this in such a manner that these pupils will be content to remain in the grade or in the section where they are.

They will persuade them by means of some reward, by assigning to them some office, such, for instance, as Head of the Class, and making them understand that it is better to be the first, or among the first, in a lower grade than the last in a more advanced one.

ARTICLE II

Section I

Charts of the Alphabet and of Syllables: What They Should Contain, and the Manner of Arranging the Pupils Who Are Reading Them

Those pupils who have not yet learned to read will not make use of a reading book until they begin to be able to spell well syllables of two and of three letters.

For this subject in the first class, there will be two large charts attached to the wall, the tops of the charts being about six or seven feet above the floor. One of these charts will be composed of single letters, both capitals and small letters, diphthongs and letters joined together; and the other of syllables of two and of three letters.*

The benches of the pupils who are reading from these charts should be neither too near nor too far away for the readers to be able to see and read the letters and syllables easily. For this reason care must be taken that the front of the first bench should be at least four feet distant from the wall to which the charts are attached.

For the same reason the pupils who are studying these charts will be seated facing them, in such a manner that if, for instance, there are twenty-four who are learning the alphabet and twelve who are learning to read syllables, and each bench will seat twelve pupils, they will be seated upon three benches placed one behind the other, eight of those who are learning the alphabet and four of those who are

---

* The models of these two charts are given at the end of Part II.

learning to read syllables upon each bench. The same proportions will be maintained in case the benches will seat fewer or more pupils or if there be a larger or smaller number studying one or the other of these two charts.

Section II

Method of Reading the Alphabet

All the pupils who are reading the alphabet will have for each lesson only one line of the capital or of the small letters, and they will not read the following line until they know well the one that they have to learn. However, in order that they may not forget the preceding lines that they have learned, they will follow attentively and repeat in a low voice the letters that are being pronounced by the pupil who is reading aloud. Each pupil of this class will read over alone and privately at least three times all the capital and all the small letters of the line which he has for his lesson, reading them once in the regular order and twice out of order, so that they may not be learned only by rote.

When a pupil does not know the name of a letter, if it is a small letter, the teacher will show him the capital letter of the same name; and if he does not know either of them, some other pupil who knows it well will be asked to name it. Sometimes even, the teacher may call upon a pupil who is not in the same grade; and he will never allow a pupil to call one letter by the name of another more than once: to say b, q, p, for d, for instance, and similarly for others.

When a pupil finds it difficult to remember a letter, he will be required to repeat it several times in succession, and he will not proceed to the next line until he knows this letter perfectly as well as the others.

When a pupil has learned all the lines of the alphabet chart, before beginning the syllables, he will continue until the end of the month to study the entire alphabet, of which he will be required to read all the letters at random, in order to ascertain whether he knows them all; and he will not advance further until he does know them perfectly.

It is necessary to observe that it is of very great importance that a pupil should not cease to study the alphabet before he knows it perfectly; for otherwise he will never be able to read well, and the teachers who will later be in charge of him will have great difficulty.

The pupils who are learning to read the alphabet will observe and follow those who are learning the syllables throughout all the time that they are reading their lessons, and, likewise, those who are reading the syllables will observe and follow during the time of the lessons on the alphabet.

Throughout all the lessons on the alphabet and the syllables, the teacher will always indicate with the pointer the letters and syllables which he wishes pronounced.

The teacher will take care that the pupils when reading pronounce well all the letters, especially those that are at times difficult to pronounce well, such as the following: *b, c, d, e, f, g, h, m, n, o, p, r, t, x, z*. He should apply himself particularly to the correction of bad accents that are peculiar to the locality, making them say *bé* for *b*, *cé* for *c*, *dé* for *d*, and thus with the others.

M and *n* should be pronounced like *eme* and *ene*, *x* like *icce*, *y* like *i*; *z* should be pronounced like *zede*, *æ* and *œ* like *e* and not as though these letters were separated *a, e* and *o, e.*

The letters *i* and *u* can be consonants as well as vowels. When they stand alone before one or two other vowels without consonants, they are pronounced otherwise than when they are vowels. The consonant *i* is written with a tail, thus: *j;* and the consonant *u* is written with a point at the bottom, thus: *v.*

The consonant *i* is pronounced like *gi,* and the consonant *u* like *vé,* this being done in order to distinguish them from the vowels *i* and *u* in pronunciation as well as in writing.

All the letters of the alphabet should be pronounced very distinctly and separately, with a distinct pause after each one.

The teacher will take care that a pupil, when reading, should open his mouth well and that he should not pronounce the letters between his teeth (which is a very great fault), that he should speak neither too rapidly nor too slowly nor with any tone or manner that savors of affectation but with a very natural one. He will also allow no pupil to raise his voice too much when reciting his lesson. It suffices that he who is reading should be heard by all those of the same grade.

The letters joined together must also be pronounced very distinctly, each one separately, as though in fact each one were separated from the others. For instance, to pronounce *ct,* first, *c* must be pronounced alone and then, after a little pause, *t.* The same should be done with the other groups.

STUDIES

Section III

Method of Reading the Chart of Syllables

The pupils will be made to read the chart of syllables one after another in order, just as they would read a lesson in a book; and the teacher will always indicate the syllable with the pointer.

Each pupil will read at least three lines. All that has been said in reference to the alphabet on the subject of pronouncing well and very distinctly all the letters must also be carefully observed in reading syllables.

The teacher will see that the pupils do not read the syllables in too rapid succession, but that, while making a short pause between the letters of a syllable, they make a longer one after each syllable, taking care not to allow them to repeat several syllables together and too rapidly.

There are three letters which present special difficulties in respect to pronunciation; these are *c*, *g*, and *t*. When *c*, comes before *a*, *o*, or *u*, it is pronounced like *q*, unless there be a tail or comma under the *c*, thus: *ç*, for then it is pronounced like *s* as well as when it comes before *e* or *i*.

In the same manner, when *g* is found before *a*, *o*, or *u*, it must be sounded as though there were a *u* between them, so that the three syllables *ga*, *go*, *gu* are pronounced in French *gua*, *guo*, *gue*. When *g* is placed before *e* or *i* it is called soft *g*, and it is pronounced like the consonant *j*; for instance, the syllables *ge* and *gi* are sounded like *je* and *ji*. When *t* is found before *i*, and this *i* is followed by another vowel, the *t* is pronounced like *c*; for example, the word *prononciation* is pronounced as though it were written *prononciacion;* and thus with others.

73

CONDUCT OF THE SCHOOLS

THE PRIMER

The first book which the pupils of the Christian Schools will learn to read will be composed of all sorts of French syllables of two, three, four, five, six, and seven letters and of some words to facilitate the pronunciation of the syllables. Ordinarily two pages will be assigned for each lesson.

The beginners should not read less than two lines, and the others not less than three, according to the number of pupils and the time that the teacher has in which to make them read. As soon as any pupil begins this grade, in order that he may accustom himself to read his book while the others are reading, the teacher will take care to assign to him, for as many days as he may need him, a companion who, when the others are reading, will teach him by following and making him follow in the same book, which both will hold, one on one side and the other on the other. The pupils will only spell the syllables in the primer and will not read them. It will be necessary to make them understand first the difficulties which are to be met in the pronunciation of syllables, and which are not slight in French. For this reason, each teacher must know perfectly the little treatise on pronunciation.

In order to teach spelling well, it is necessary to have all the letters pronounced in the same tone and very distinctly, so that the sound of each one can be fully heard separately from the others, and to have the syllables pronounced in the same manner. Thus, he who is spelling should make each syllable completely and distinctly heard before beginning to

74

spell the following one, and he should pronounce them almost as separately as if there were commas between them. For instance, to spell well the syllable *quo,* each letter must be named separately and distinctly: *q, u, o;* also *c, a, r; t, a, r* —and not quickly and together: *quo, car, tar.* This practice is of very great importance, and there is even more to be feared from, and much more inconvenience in, spelling and reading too rapidly when reciting lessons than too slowly.

ARTICLE IV

THE FIRST BOOK

The first book which will be used in the Christian Schools will be a continuous narrative. Those who read in it will only spell, and they will always be given one page for each lesson.

Each pupil will spell about three lines at least, depending upon the time that the teacher has at his disposal and upon the number of the pupils. The teacher will take care that those who are in this grade distinguish and separate one from another the syllables of the words, that they do not put into the first syllable a letter which should be in the second one, and likewise with the others; for instance, in spelling the word *déclare,* they should not say *déc-lare* but should say *dé-clare;* and the same with other words.

The teacher will see that they pronounce all the syllables of a word as they should be pronounced in this word and not as they would be pronounced if they were separated one from another and in different words. For example, the syllable *son* is [not] pronounced in the word *personne* by sounding the *n* as it is always sounded in the word *son* when this syllable alone forms the word which signifies sound; for then so much stress is not placed upon the *n*. In the same way, in the word *louppe* the first syllable is pronounced otherwise than is *loup* when it forms the word which signifies the animal; for in the first word, *louppe*, the *p* is sounded in the first syllable, whereas in the second word, *loup*, the *p* is not sounded, and it is pronounced as if there were only *lou*. The teacher will take care that those who are in this grade pronounce the words as though they were standing alone, paying no attention either to the preceding word or to the following one. For instance, in the following sentence: *Ne pensez point à ce que vous aurez à dire*, they will pronounce the word *point* as they would pronounce it when alone and not followed by a vowel. Thus they will not pronounce the *t* but will pronounce the word as though it were only *poin*, naming, however, all the letters as follows: *p, o, i, n, t.*

Likewise in the word *vous*, they will name all the letters: *v, o, u, s*, but they will pronounce it as though there were no *s* and will say *v, o, u, s, vou*. They will do the same in the word *aurez*, not pronouncing the *z*, but, after naming all the letters of the second syllable, *rez*, they will say, as though there were no *z, ré*, with an accent on the *é*, paying no attention, in case of either of these words, to the vowels which follow them.

The Second Book

The second book which will be used in the Christian Schools will be a book of Christian instructions. The pupils will not study this book unless they can spell perfectly without hesitating.

There will be two kinds of readers of this book: those who spell and read by syllables and those who do not spell but only read by syllables.

All will have the same lesson, and while one is spelling or reading, all the others will follow, both those who spell and read and those who only read. Those who both spell and read will do nothing but spell in the morning. In the afternoon they will spell first, and, after all of them have spelled, they will read without distinction together with those who do nothing but read. If those who only read are in the same class with those who both spell and read, while the latter are spelling, they will only follow. The teacher will take care from time to time to require some of them unexpectedly to spell some words, in order to ascertain whether they are following attentively.

All those who read in this book will read only by syllables, that is to say, with a pause of equal length between each syllable, without paying any attention to the words which they compose: for instance, *Con-stan-tin, Em-pe-reur, as-sis-ta, au con-ci-le, de, Ni-cé-e,* and so on. If these two kinds of readers are in different classes, those who do nothing but read will all spell about one line at most for each one, every day in the afternoon before any one of them begins to read.

Those who spell will spell about three lines and will read afterward as much as they have spelled. Those who only read will read five or six lines, according to the number of pupils and the time which the teacher may have.

The Third Book

The third book which will be used to teach reading in the Christian Schools will be one upon which the Brothers Directors and the Brother Superior of the Institute in each place will agree.

All who read from this book will do so by sentences and in sequence, stopping only at periods and at commas. Only those who know how to read perfectly by syllables without fail will be in this grade. Two or three pages will be given for a lesson each time, from one full stop to another: a chapter, an article, or a section.

The beginners will read about eight lines; and the more advanced, twelve or fifteen lines, according to the time that the teacher has and the number of the pupils.

Those who are reading the third book will also be taught all the rules of French pronunciation, both how to pronounce syllables and words perfectly correctly and how to sound the consonants at the end of words when the following word begins with a vowel. The teacher will teach the pupils all these things while they are reading, calling their attention to all the mistakes in pronunciation which they make, and he will correct them carefully without overlooking any.

ARTICLE VII

Charts of Vowels and Consonants, of Punctuation and Accents, and of Numerals

The pupils who are studying the third book will be taught to recognize the vowels and the consonants and to distinguish them from each other. They will be taught the reason why the ones are called vowels and the others consonants. They will also be instructed concerning the pauses that must be made at a period, at a colon, at a semicolon, at a comma, and the difference between, and the reasons for, these signs.

They will be taught the significance of an interrogation mark, of an exclamation mark, of parentheses, of a hyphen, of the two dots over an *ë*, an *ï*, or a *ü*, and the reason why all these are used; the different abbreviations and their meaning; the three different accents, the reasons for which they are used and what they signify. They will likewise be taught to read the numerals, both Arabic and Roman, up to one hundred thousand, at least, and in various combinations. There must be for this purpose in each classroom two charts, upon one of which will be shown separately the vowels and consonants, and above each consonant will be indicated the syllable which is pronounced in naming this consonant. On this chart will also be the different punctuation marks for words and sentences, that is to say, the apostrophe, parentheses, the hyphen, the two dots over *ë*, *ï*, or *ü*, the three different accents, and the abbreviations of words in all the forms in which they may be found. The other chart will contain the Arabic and Roman numerals, separately and in columns, up to the number one hundred thousand at least.

One half hour in the afternoon twice each week, at the beginning of the lesson in the third book, will be taken to teach these things.

On the first day of the week, there will be taught during this half hour all that is on the first chart and in the following manner:

The teacher will make several pupils, one after another,

recite and explain different things which he will point out on the chart.

While one pupil is explaining, the others will look at the chart and will be attentive, so that they may understand and retain what is being said.

The teacher will take care from time to time to question some other pupils on the same subject, in order to ascertain whether they are applying themselves to what their companion is saying and whether they understand it.

The numerals will be taught in the same manner in the afternoon of the day following a holiday or of the third school day, if there is no holiday in the week. In places where there are only two classes, they will be recited on Fridays instead of arithmetic by the pupils of the writing class.*

ARTICLE VIII

READING OF LATIN

The book by means of which the reading of Latin will be taught is the Psalter. Only those who know perfectly how to read French will be taught this subject. There will be three sections of readers of Latin: the beginners, who will read only by syllables; the intermediate, who will begin to read with pauses; and the advanced, who will read with pauses without making any mistakes whatsoever.

Only those who are able to read by syllables perfectly will be made to read with pauses. Both the readers by syllables and those who read with pauses will have the same lesson,

* The models of these two charts are given at the end of Part II.

but they will read separately. However, the ones will follow while the others are reading.

Those who are learning to read Latin will read both in the morning and in the afternoon, except on the days when they study the vowels and numerals. On these days they will not read in the afternoon after having read in the third book.

Those who are learning to write will read only Latin in the morning and French in the afternoon. Only about two pages will be assigned as a lesson each day. The readers by syllables will read about six lines; and those who read with pauses, about ten lines. The teacher will take care to teach the pupils who are beginning to read Latin the manner of pronouncing it correctly, which differs in several respects from the pronunciation of French. He will make them understand above all that all the letters are pronounced in Latin and that all the syllables which begin with *q* or *g* are pronounced otherwise than in French—as is indicated at the end of the treatise on pronunciation.

The teacher will teach the pupils those things which concern Latin pronunciation while they are reading, as has been indicated in respect to French.

ARTICLE IX

THE BOOK ON CHRISTIAN CIVILITY

When the pupils know how to read French perfectly and are in the third section of Latin reading, they will be taught to write, and they will be taught to read the book on Christian Civility.

This book contains all the duties of children, both toward God and toward their parents, and the rules of civil and

Christian decorum. It is printed in Gothic characters, which are more difficult to read than French characters.

They will not spell, and they will not read by syllables in this book; but all those to whom it is given will read always consecutively and with pauses.

This book will be read only in the morning. For each lesson will be assigned one chapter or as far as the first division or asterisk. The beginners will read at least four lines; and the more advanced, at least ten lines.

When the pupils are in the fourth section of round-hand writing or are beginning the third section of slanting writing, they will be taught to read papers or parchments written by hand. At first, they will be given the easiest to read, then less easy ones, afterward more difficult ones, in measure as they advance, and so on until they are capable of reading the most difficult writing that they may encounter.

No pupil will be permitted to bring from home any manuscript to read in school without the order of the Brother Director. Each teacher of the writing class should know perfectly how to read all kinds of papers written by hand. Above all, he should have read and studied well those which are in the classroom, and the Brother Director should make sure that he knows how to read them perfectly.

As those manuscripts which are of equal difficulty are ordinarily written by the same person—especially those consisting of only one sheet or leaf, such as writs, receipts, and notes of hand—it is very useful to have the pupils learn at once to read all the writings of any one writer, so that, the form of his characters and his abbreviations having impressed themselves on their memories, they will have no further difficulty in reading them. By this means, the most difficult and confused writing will become very easy for them.

Manuscripts will be read twice a week, in the afternoon at the opening of school on the first and fifth school day, if there are no holy days of obligation in the week; but if there is a holy day which does not fall on a Wednesday, or if there are two holy days in the week, they will be read on the first and fourth school day.

The pupils will read one after another, and they will come in turn, two by two, before the teacher, in the order in which they are seated on the benches, so that all those of one bench will come in succession, and then those of the next bench or the one behind it.

The beginners will read about thirty words. Those of the more advanced sections will read about ten words more than those of the preceding section. Thus the amount read will be increased by ten words for each successive section.

CHAPTER IV

WRITING

ARTICLE I

GENERAL CONSIDERATIONS

It is necessary that the pupils should know how to read perfectly well both French and Latin before they are taught to write.

If, however, it should happen that there be any who have reached the age of twelve years and have not yet begun to write, they may begin writing at the same time that they begin Latin, provided they know how to read French well and correctly, and it be presumed that they will not come to school for a long enough time to learn to write sufficiently well. This is a matter to which the Brother Director and the Inspector of Schools will attend.

ARTICLE II

WRITING MATERIALS

Section I

Paper

The teacher will take care that the pupils always have white paper for school use. For this reason, he will instruct them to ask their parents for some, at the latest whenever they have no more than six white sheets left. He will see that they bring each time at least half a quire of good paper, not too coarse, too gray, or too heavy, but white, smooth, well dried, and well glazed and, above all, that will not absorb ink easily; for this is a great defect and a great hindrance in writing. Neither will he permit any pupil to bring loose paper or that the paper be folded in quarters: the sheets must be sewed together their entire length.

Finally, he will take care that the pupils keep their paper always very clean, neither crumpled nor turned down at the corners. There will be in the school a chest or a cupboard, in which all paper and other school material will be put.

The officers of the writing class, who will distribute and collect the papers in turn, will take care to do so with order and in silence, and they will be careful not to mix the papers.

Section II

Pens and Penknives

The teacher will oblige the writers to bring to school each day at least two large quills, so that they may always be able to write with one of them while the other is being trimmed.

He will see that the quills are neither too slender nor too thick, but round, strong, clear, dry, and of the second growth. He will take care that the pens be clean and not full of ink, not bitten at the end or trimmed too short, and that the pupils do not put the point of their pens in their mouths or leave them lying about. Writers of the third section should also have penknives, so that they may learn to trim their pens.

All the writers will also have writing cases in which to put their pens and penknives. The teacher will require that they be the longest that can be found, in order that the pupils may not be obliged to cut their pens too short, which would prevent them from writing well.

Section III

Ink

The pupils will be supplied with ink. For this purpose, there will be as many inkwells as possible. They will be made of lead, so that they cannot be overturned, and one will be placed between each two pupils. The teacher will see that ink is put into them when needed and that the pupils who are appointed to collect the papers clean the inkwells once a week, on the last school day. There will be no cotton in these inkwells, only ink, which will be supplied gratuitously.

The teacher will see that the pupils ink their pens carefully, dipping only the point of the pen and then shaking it gently in the inkwell and not on the floor.

Section IV

Models

There will be two kinds of models given to the pupils. The first will consist of two alphabets: one of letters not joined and one of letters joined together; the second of models in lines, each one of which will contain five or six lines.

The models which are given to the pupils will be written on loose sheets, and the teachers will not write any on their

papers or any large capital letters or strokes at the be
of their pages. This is a matter of importance.

All the models in lines will consist of sentences from Ho.,
Scripture or of Christian maxims taken from the works of
the Fathers or from devotional books.

For this purpose, there will be in each school two collections: one of sentences from Holy Scripture, both the Old
and the New Testament; the other of maxims of piety taken
from some good books.

The teachers will give no models that are not taken from
one of these two collections, and they will make special use
of those taken from Holy Scripture, which should make a
greater impression and more easily touch the heart, as it is
the word of God.

Section V

Transparents and Blotting Paper

Transparents will be given only to such pupils as are unable to write straight without lines. The Inspector of Schools
and the teacher will examine those who may need them, and
they will make the least possible use of them.

A transparent is a sheet of paper with lines drawn across
it at proper intervals. It is called a transparent because when
it is placed beneath the sheet upon which is to be written,
the lines are visible through the latter and serve to guide the
lines of writing.

Each one of the writers will have with his paper a sheet or
two of coarse paper which easily absorbs ink and which they
will place on the page which they have written, in order to

87

dry it without blotting. It is called blotting paper on account of the use that is made of it.

Time Devoted to Writing in School and Amount to Be Written by Each Pupil

The pupils will spend one hour in writing, both in the morning and in the afternoon: in the morning from eight until nine o'clock, and in the afternoon from three until four. From the beginning of November until the end of January, they will begin to write in the afternoon at half past two o'clock and will finish at half past three. Should it happen that some pupils will be coming to school only for a short time longer and that they need to write for a longer period than the others in order to learn to write sufficiently well, they may be permitted to write during school hours, except during the time devoted to the reading of manuscripts, to prayers, and to Catechism, provided, however, that they know how to read French, Latin, and the Christian Civility so well that they would derive no further benefit from reading them; that they read in their turn during all lessons; that they also take their turn in reciting the Catechism, the responses of Holy Mass, the prayers during breakfast and lunch; and that they have been writing lines for at least six months. This will, however, be granted to none without the orders of the Brother Director. Each pupil will write at least two pages a day: one in the morning and the other in the afternoon.

WRITING

DIFFERENT SECTIONS OF PUPILS WRITING ROUND HAND

There will be six sections of writers of round hand, distinguished one from another by the different things which are taught the pupils in each of them.

The first section will consist of those who are learning to hold the pen and the body correctly and to make with ease the straight and circular movements. The teacher will not concern himself with them other than to see that they hold their pens, their bodies and their hands correctly, and that they make these two movements well. It is very important that pupils should not begin to write until they have learned to hold their pens correctly and have acquired a free movement of the fingers.

The second section of writers will consist of those who are learning to form the five letters *C, O, I, F, M* and who, for this purpose, will write one page of each of these letters, one after another. In respect to the pupils of these two sections, the teacher will take care only to see often that they form the letters properly, that they join them together neatly and as they should be, and that they place them correctly. Before putting them in the third section, he will teach them the letters which are based upon *O, I, F* and the manner of forming the derivatives on these three letters.

The third section will consist of those who are learning to form correctly all the letters of the alphabet, and, for this purpose, they should write one page of each letter one after another. When the teacher considers it expedient, he will have them write a line composed of each letter.

The fourth section will consist of those who, in addition to perfecting themselves in those things which the two preceding sections should learn, are learning to place the letters properly and evenly, as they should be when in the same line, and to extend the long letters as much as they should be above or below the body of the writing, according to the rules of penmanship. To this effect, the pupils of this section will write the whole alphabet joined together on each line. They will be required to apply the same rules that should be observed for a long word which would fill an entire line.

The fifth section will consist of all who are writing sentences in large letters, such as are used in accounts, so long as they continue to write in these characters. They should write at first one page of each line of their models, one line after another; and when the teacher, in agreement with the Brother Director, considers it expedient, they will copy the entire model. Their models will be changed every month. They will also write on the reverse side of their papers the entire alphabet joined together on each line, until they know how to write it perfectly, and then they will be required to copy their models of a connected sentence on all the pages of their paper.

The sixth section will consist of those who are writing sentences in these same large letters of accounts on the obverse of their paper and in commercial hand on the reverse.

WRITING

DIFFERENT SECTIONS OF PUPILS WRITING ITALIAN SCRIPT

When the pupils begin to learn to write Italian script, they will be required to observe all that is indicated above in connection with the first and the following sections in round hand.

There will be also six sections of writers of Italian script.

The first section will consist of those who are learning how to hold the pen and the entire body in a proper position, and they will not be permitted to write until they have acquired a complete movement of the thumb and the fingers.

The second section will consist of those who are learning to form the five letters *C, O, I, F, M* and who should write one page of each letter, as has been indicated for the second section in round hand.

The third section will consist of those who are being taught the manner of forming correctly the letters of the alphabet, their proper position and slant. For this purpose, they will write one page of each letter joined together one after another. Afterward, the teacher, in agreement with the Brother Director, will have them write one line of each letter, provided they have made progress in this section.

The fourth section in Italian script will consist of those who are being taught the relative proportions of the letters, the distance that should separate them, and the space that there should be between the lines.

They must also be trained in this section to write with firmness and to pass easily from one letter to another. The pupils in this section will write the entire alphabet in regular order on each line.

In the fifth section, the pupils will write sentences formed of large characters, in the same manner as has been indicated for the fifth section in round hand.

And those of the sixth section will write sentences formed of large characters on the obverse of their paper, and on the reverse they will write in small characters. In these last two sections, the teacher and the pupils will apply the same rules as in the fifth and sixth sections of the writers of round hand.

If a pupil who is beginning to learn to write Italian script has one year, that is to say eleven months, in which to learn it, he will be taught during the first month how to hold his pen and his body and to make with ease the straight and circular movements, as is indicated above. The first two months afterward, he will write one page of each letter joined together. The two following months, he will write one line of each letter joined together. During the next two months, the entire alphabet in order on each line. The last four months, he will write sentences in medium-sized letters.

In respect to pupils who will thus have little time to learn to write, their time will be distributed in the manner indicated above, in proportion to the time which they have at their disposal for this purpose; and they will, of necessity, be advanced at the end of the assigned period of time, whether they do or do not know what they should know in order to be advanced.

The teacher will, however, take pains to continue to teach them, during the advanced lessons, what pertains to the preceding ones, in case they do not know it completely.

WRITING

Correct Position of the Body

The teacher will take care that the pupils always hold their bodies as erect as possible, only slightly inclined but without touching the table, so that, with the elbow placed on the table, the chin can be rested upon the hand. The body must be somewhat turned and free on the same side. The teacher will require them to observe all else concerning the position of the body that is according to the rules of penmanship.

He will take care above all that they do not hold their right arms too far from their bodies and that they do not press their stomachs against the table; for, besides being very ungraceful, this posture might cause them great inconvenience. In order to make him hold his body correctly, the teacher will himself place the pupil in the posture which he should maintain, with each limb where it should be. Whenever he sees a pupil change this position, he will take care to put him back into it.

ARTICLE VII

Correct Method of Holding the Pen and Position of Paper

The second thing of which the teacher should be careful in regard to writing is to teach how to hold the pen and to place the paper. This is of great importance, for pupils who have not been trained in the beginning to hold their pens correctly will never write well.

In order to teach the manner of holding the pen properly, it is necessary to arrange the hand of the pupil and put the pen between his fingers.

It will be useful and fitting, when the pupils begin to write, to give them a stick of the thickness of a pen and on which there are three grooves, two on the right and one on the left, which indicate the places where the three fingers should be placed, so as to teach them to hold the pen in their fingers properly and to make them acquire a good position of these three fingers.

Care must be taken that they place the three fingers on these three grooves and that, during a fortnight at least, they apply themselves in school at writing time to rendering their fingers supple by means of this stick or of an unpointed pen. The teacher will urge them to do it then and later, as often as possible, at home and everywhere else. In respect to the two other fingers, which should be under the pen, it would be well to have the pupils tie them, during as long a time as is necessary, in the position in which they should be held. Concerning the position of the paper, it should be placed straight, and to this the teacher will pay great attention; for if the paper is slanting, the lines will be slanting, and the body cannot be held in a good position, nor can the letters be so well formed.

ARTICLE VIII

METHOD OF TRAINING TO WRITE WELL

As soon as a pupil begins to write and is in the second or third section, the teacher will show him how to form the letters, where to begin them, when to ease the pressure on the pen, and when to raise it. He must do this several times. Afterward, he will make him understand the manner of doing all these things correctly.

In order that the pupils may observe carefully and apprehend well the form of the letters, he will guide their hands from time to time and for as long a time as he judges needful; but he will do this only with those who are in the first and the second section of writers.

He will let them write alone for some time after he has guided their hands and shown them how to form the letters. However, from time to time, he will examine what they have written.

He will then have them practice making, and will help them to make, the connections between letters in an easy manner by lessening the pressure on the pen slightly on the side next to the thumb. He will take care that they always do this in the same way.

He will also take care, when the pupils are writing the alphabet, that they do not crowd or space too much either the letters or the lines. As soon as they are in the second grade of writing, he will give them transparents, to accustom them to writing their lines straight, and he will see that they place the bottom of the body of the letters on the line of the transparent.

He will, however, not let them make use of the transparents continually, but will take them away from time to time, permitting them to write five or six lines without using them, in order that they may imperceptibly accustom themselves to writing straight of their own accord and without this aid. Those who are writing in lines will use transparents as little as possible.

It is important not to have the pupils write in lines until they know how to form all the letters properly and to write the entire alphabet in all the manners which are indicated for the different sections in writing. One may be sure that by keeping to this practice the pupils will make more progress in one month than they would otherwise make in six.

The teacher will not permit the pupils to write anything other than what is on their models.

When the Teacher Will Trim the Pens of the Pupils. Time and Manner of Teaching the Pupils to Trim Them

The teacher will trim the pens of the pupils when they need it, but only during the writing periods.

To this effect, the pupils who need to have their pens trimmed will take care to place them before them, so that, when he comes to correct their writing, the teacher may perceive them. They will remain uncovered until he has returned them, and when receiving them they will kiss his hand and bow low to him. They will not cease writing while the teacher is trimming their pens.

As soon as a pupil has been writing for one month at the most in the third section, the teacher will oblige him to trim his pens for himself and will teach him how to do this. To this effect, he will make him come near and will show him in the following manner all that is necessary to do it properly:

For this purpose, he will take a new quill and will teach

the pupil how to strip it of feathers without tearing it and how to straighten it if it is bent. Second, how to hold it in his fingers. Third, how to open the stem, both at the back and the front. Fourth, how to hold the quill to slit it. Fifth, with what and how to slit it. Sixth, how it should be slit, both for round hand and for Italian and running hand. Seventh, how to hollow it and that to do this the point of the penknife must be used. Eighth, that for running hand the two angles of the point must be equal, while for other styles of writing one of the angles should be wider and longer, and the other thinner and shorter. Ninth, which side should be wider and longer. Tenth, which side should be thinner and shorter. Eleventh, how to open it, how long and deep the opening should be, and with what part of the blade of the penknife it should be made. Twelfth, how to clear the point and to cut it with the middle of the blade. Thirteenth, how to hold the penknife, whether it should be held upright or flat. Fourteenth, finally, that it should not be cut on the nail of the left thumb, on the table, or on wood but on the stem of another quill introduced into the one which is being cut. Then, the teacher will explain to the pupil all the terms used in reference to trimming pens: for instance, what is called an angle, a point, and so on, and he will make him repeat them.

In order to make the pupils understand, retain, and practice all that pertains to the proper way of trimming pens, the teacher will himself trim a new pen in the presence of the pupil on three successive days. He will make him understand all that he does in trimming it and why he does it. Immediately afterward, he will make him trim another one, telling him all that he must do and how to do it well and correcting him when he fails in anything. This he will continue to do for about a week.

INSPECTION OF WRITERS AND CORRECTION OF WRITING

It is necessary that the teacher should inspect all the writers every day and, in the case of beginners, even two or three times a day. He must observe whether the pens of those who trim their own pens are well trimmed; whether their bodies are in a correct posture; whether their paper is straight and clean; whether they hold their pens properly; whether they have models; whether they are writing as much as they should; whether they are trying to do well; whether they are not writing too fast; whether they are making their lines straight; whether they are placing all their letters in the same position and at a proper distance; whether the body of all the letters is of the same height and in the same character, and the letters are distinct and well formed; whether the words and the lines are not too close together or too far apart. At each inspection, he will correct the writing of one-half of the writers. In this manner, he will correct all of them, in the morning as well as in the afternoon without fail.

He will pass behind them, one after another; and for this reason there will be some space between the benches of the writers. He will place himself at the right side of the one whom he is to correct, and he will show him all the mistakes which he has made in writing, in the posture of the body as well as in the manner of holding the pen and forming the letters, and in all the other things which he should examine when he inspects the writers and which are indicated above.

When, in correcting, he speaks of hangers, feet, heads, tails, members and bodies of letters, of divisions, distance, separations, of height, width, curve, semicurve, thick and fine, small character, large character, etc., he will explain all these terms, each one in particular, and will afterward ask the explanation, saying, for instance, "What is meant by hangers?"

He will take care that the pupils be attentive when he corrects their writing. He will mark with a slight stroke of the pen the principal mistakes that they have made, but will take care in the beginning not to call their attention to more than three or four mistakes, for fear of confusing them if he should show them a greater number and making them forget what he has taught them, on account of the confusion which the greater number of mistakes for which they had been reproved would create in their minds.

When he thus corrects the writing, he will show the pupils how he forms the syllables or the letters which he writes to correct them; and, in order that they may apply themselves afterwards to forming them in the same manner, after having written them at the top or on the margin of their papers, he will make them write a line of each letter or syllable which he has corrected and two lines of each word. If they have not the time to do all this on that day, he will charge them to finish the next day before beginning to copy the model; and if they do not yet succeed even after that, he will oblige them to write, during all the time they have for writing, only the letters, syllables, or words which they have written incorrectly, two or three times in succession. When he is correcting the writing of the pupils, the teacher will not write on their papers any lines or words of several syllables. It will suffice that he write the letter which the pupil has written badly; and if the latter has failed in connecting some letters, let the teacher write the two letters joined together or the syllable at the very most.

While he is inspecting and correcting the writing of some of the pupils, he will be careful to keep all the others always in sight, in order to observe all that takes place in the class; and if he finds anyone at fault, he will warn him by making a sign. He will watch particularly over those who have most need of it, that is to say, the beginners and the negligent. He will take care above all during this time that nothing escape his eye.

He will also pay very particular attention to those who are making the two straight and circular movements. He will notice whether their pens are not slipping out of their fingers, and he will replace them as they should be, explaining what should be done to keep them so; whether, in making the movements, they do not move the arm instead of extending and bending only the fingers; whether they have more difficulty in moving their fingers than their arms; whether the thumb always moves first; whether they do not rest the hand when making these movements; whether they do not press down when making them, instead of making them lightly. He will indicate to them the mistakes that they may have made in these things and the means of correcting them, by showing them how they must bend and extend their fingers, how they should rest the arm without pressing it too much on the table, how they should write from one side of their paper to the other, touching the paper only slightly with the point of the pen and lightly gliding the arm from side to side, from left to right.

In regard to the straight movement, he will be careful that they draw straight from top to bottom, that they do not hold the fingers too stiffly, but bend them as much as is necessary to make the movement well, and that they keep the pen always level without varying, either in ascending or in descending. In regard to the circular movement, he will observe whether they begin it at the bottom and at the top with the same facility, as well from left to right as from right to left; and whether they do not hold their fingers too stiffly and their arms fixed on the table. From time to time, he will watch the pupils of the first section make these two movements, in order to see for himself the mistakes which they make in respect to all the above-mentioned things. At the same time, he will indicate to them the means of correcting them, and he will make them correct them at once.

The teacher will call the attention of the pupils of the second and third sections—and even of the following ones —to mistakes in the manner of forming letters, for instance, whether a *B* in round hand which a pupil has made is too much inclined to one side or to the other; whether it is curved or humped; whether all its dimensions are correct—that is to say, whether it has the proper height (which should be twice that of the body of the writing, that is, eight points of the pen), whether it is too high, whether it has the width that it should at the top and at the bottom —whether it lacks some of its parts; whether the full strokes or the fine ones are where they should be. He will do the same in respect to all the other letters, and he will mark, with a stroke of the pen at each place, all the mistakes that they have made in forming these letters. For example, if the *b* is too much inclined to the right, he will mark it in this manner: ƀ ; if too much inclined to the left, he will mark it thus: ꝑ. He will call the attention of those of the third and of the following sections to all the mistakes which they may have made in respect to connections: whether they have failed to make any where they should have been made; whether they have made any where they should not have been made; whether they have begun them at another point of the letter than at the one where they should start; whether they extend too high or not high enough; whether they are too thin or too thick; whether they are winding when they should be circular; whether they are straight when they should be circular; whether they have held the pen as it should be held to make them; and whether they have turned it instead of easing the pressure.

To make the pupils understand easily and very well the defects of their letters and connections, the teacher, after having shown them to them, will ask them what is wrong with the letter or the connection and why the one or the other is not good. Then he will give to the letter or the connection which the pupil has made badly the form which it should have, by writing the one or the other over the letter or the connection which the pupil has made badly. He will then ask why the one which he has retraced is good and what there is in it that was not in the letter made by the pupil. After this, he will make between the lines a letter or two joined letters, which he will have them make in the same way, and he will observe how they form it.

When the teacher has taught a pupil in the first three sections something or has corrected something for him, he will not leave him at once; but he will make him do in his presence what he has taught him or write the letters which he has corrected. The teacher will watch him, as much to see whether he holds the pen the way that he has shown him as to see whether he begins the letters properly and whether he does well what he has been taught, so that he may tell him in what he fails. If the teacher should leave him at once, the pupil would forget all that had been said or taught him. Furthermore, this will please the parents; for the children will not fail to say that the teacher has shown them by making them write before him, has guided their hand, and so on.

If a pupil fails to place the letters properly, that is to say, when they are not in conformity with each other, the teacher will draw two straight lines with the pen over the entire place in the line where the pupil has failed: one stroke from the base of the last letter which is properly placed, and the other at the top of the body of the letter, and will then explain to him in what the mistake in position consists and which the letters are that are not well placed. The teacher will do the same when the hangers are not of equal height or equally situated. To correct a defect in distance between letters, the teacher will indicate the space that there should be between the preceding letter and the following one, and he will then make a downward stroke with the pen at the point where the first member of the next letter which is too close to or too far from the preceding one should be placed.

To correct a defect in distance between two words that are either too close together or too far apart, the teacher will make an *m* of the width of seven times that of the point of the pen, which is the space that should be between two words. If there is a period between the words, the teacher will make five hangers of an *m* joined together, of the width of thirteen times that of the point of the pen, which is the space that should be between two words separated by a period. If there is a comma, a colon, or a semicolon, he will make between the two words two *n*'s of ten times the width of that of the point of the pen, which is the distance at which they should be from each other.

To correct a defect in distance between lines, in order to make the pupil note what distance there should be between the two lines, the teacher will make four bodies of letters joined together on the margin of the paper, between the lines which are either too close together or too far apart. He will make, for instance, four *o*'s joined together of the width of sixteen times that of the point of the pen. To make them acquire lightness and avoid lack of boldness in writing, the teacher will take care that the pupils do not press on their paper, just touching it with the point of the pen, almost without feeling it, and that they do not write too slowly. He will point out to them that this defect comes from holding the arm as though fixed on the table, from not bending the fingers and imparting to them the movement that they should have, or from leaning the body too much or even bending it over the table.

To make a pupil correct himself of these faults, if he is slow, he must be urged to write fast, without resting his arm on the table, placing on it only the tips of the two sustaining fingers and without paying any attention to whether he forms his letters well or badly, taking pains only to make him acquire boldness and ease of movement.

If it is a pupil who is naturally quick, it will be necessary only to arrange his hand, his arm and his body, and, after having taught him what he should do, let him write by himself, restraining him, however, and moderating him if he is too active.

To make all sorts of pupils acquire freedom and ease of movement, the teacher will show them how to pass properly from one letter to another—such as from an *i* to an *f*, from a *c* to an *l*, from an *o* to an *i*—without interruption and without raising the pen; and to correct the mistakes which they may have made in all things pertaining both to boldness and to ease of movement, he will do himself, in their presence, what he wishes them to do in order to correct themselves. After this, he will make them do what he has just done and what they had done badly.

CHAPTER V

ARITHMETIC

In the study of arithmetic, there will be pupils of different grades. Some of them will be learning addition, others subtraction, multiplication, or division, according to how advanced they may be. The teacher will take care to write on the board an example for each operation every Saturday, or on the last school day if Saturday is a holy day. He will see that all who are learning arithmetic write down their examples on Monday morning at the beginning of the writing lesson, or on the first school day if there is a holy day on Monday. To this effect, they must have a notebook of paper folded in quarters. Arithmetic will be taught only to those who are entering the fourth section in writing, and it pertains to the Brother Director or to the Inspector of Schools to promote to this study as well as to the others. Arithmetic will be taught on Tuesday and Friday, from half past one until half past two in the afternoon. If there is a holy day on Tuesday, it will be taught on Wednesday, unless there is a holy day on Monday as well as on Tuesday. If there is a holy day on Friday, it will be taught on Saturday.

To teach arithmetic, the teacher will remain seated on his chair or will stand before it, and a student of each operation will stand before him and do the example which he has for his lesson, indicating with the pointer the figures, one after another, adding, subtracting, multiplying, or dividing them aloud.

Thus, to make an addition properly, he will begin with the deniers * and always at the top, and will say, for example, 10 and 6 make 16, and so on.

While a pupil is doing the example of his lesson, the teacher will ask him several questions concerning it, in order to make him understand it better and retain it; and if he makes use of terms pertaining to the subject which the pupil does not understand, he will explain them to him and make him repeat them before going further. From time to time, the teacher will also question some other

* Denier, the smallest unit of the old French monetary system.

pupils who have the same lesson, to ascertain if they are attentive and if they understand. If the one who is doing the example fails in any respect, the teacher will make a sign to another pupil who is learning the same lesson or a more advanced lesson to correct him, which the latter will do by repeating aloud what the other one had said wrongly. If there are no lessons more advanced than this one, and if some pupil is not able to say it properly, the teacher will say it himself.

The pupil who is doing the example on the board should, when doing it, write at the bottom the result of the addition, of the subtraction, of the multiplication, or of the division and then the proof of the example which he has just done. After this, the pupil will erase all that he himself has written, but nothing more, so that another pupil may do the same example.

In arithmetic, as well as in the other subjects, it is with the most elementary examples that it will begin, and with the most advanced that it will end.

When a pupil is doing an example in arithmetic, of whatever grade it be, all the others who have the same lesson will remain seated facing the board and will pay attention to the figures that he writes and to what he says when doing his example. The pupils who are reading and who are not yet learning arithmetic will pay the same attention. The teacher will have a register of all the pupils who are learning arithmetic, divided according to the part that they are studying, and he will see that all of them do an example from their lessons on the board in school, one after another, without excepting any one of them.

On Tuesday of each week, or the first day upon which

arithmetic comes, all the pupils who are learning it and who are among the advanced students will bring, already done on their paper, the example for their lesson which the teacher has written on the board for that week, together with some others which they have invented for themselves. On Friday, they will bring a certain number of examples, from their own lessons as well as from the work of more elementary lessons, which they have done by themselves and which the teacher has assigned for them to do, according to their capacity.

During the writing time on Tuesday and Thursday afternoons, instead of correcting the writing, the teacher will correct the examples which the students of arithmetic have done by themselves on their papers. He will explain the reason why anything is incorrect, asking them, for example, concerning addition: "Why do we begin with deniers?" "Why do we reduce the deniers to sous, and the sous to livres?" * and such other similar questions as he finds that they need, and he will give them a full explanation.

CHAPTER VI

SPELLING

The teacher will take care to teach spelling to the pupils who are in the sixth section of round hand and of Italian hand. The Brother Director will see to this.

* Deniers, sous, livres may be roughly translated farthings, pence, shillings.

SPELLING

The manner of teaching them spelling will be to have them copy letters written by hand, especially such things as it may be useful for them to know how to write and of which they might later have need—such as notes of hand, receipts, agreements with workmen, legal contracts, bonds, powers of attorney, leases, deeds, official reports—in order that they may impress these things on their memories and learn to write similar ones.

After they have copied these kinds of writings for some time, the teacher will have them make and write by themselves some notes of hand, some receipts, some agreements with workmen, bills for different kinds of work done by the hour, bills for goods delivered, estimates by workmen, etc.

He will also oblige them at the same time to write what they remember of the Catechism which has been taught them during the week, especially what has been taught them on Sundays and holy days or on Wednesdays just before a holiday, if there has been no holy day in the week. If the teacher considers that some of them are unable to do this, he will have them write the lesson of the Diocesan Catechism which they have learned by heart in the past week, and which they will be obliged to write without looking at the book. For this purpose, the teacher will oblige them to have a notebook, which they will bring to him every Tuesday and Friday or any other day on which arithmetic is taught, so that he may correct the examples of arithmetic and the mistakes in spelling in what they have written. The teacher will add in his own writing the letters which they have omitted or in the places where they have put wrong ones, after having drawn a line through the latter.

The teacher will later oblige the pupils whose writing he has corrected in respect to spelling to rewrite it at home, making a fair copy just as he has corrected it; and he will take care, the next time that he corrects their spelling, to see if they have acquitted themselves of this duty.

Spelling will be taught also in the following manner: The teacher will dictate, for example, *Dieu tout puissant et miséricordieux;* all will write, and one pupil alone will spell the syllables, while writing, as follows: *Di-eu tout puis-sant et mi-sé-ri-cor-di-eux.* If he has said anything wrong in spelling—for instance, if he has said *mis* instead of *mi-sé,* etc.—the teacher or whoever is dictating will repeat the letter or the syllable that this pupil has said wrong. The one who is dictating will be careful to indicate where semicolons are to be placed.

When what has been dictated has been written, the teacher will make one pupil spell aloud what the others have written, and all the others will spell in a low voice while following.

The teacher will take care that this pupil who is spelling aloud state when there are acute or grave accents, naming the letters upon which these accents are to be placed, also when there is a period, a colon, a semicolon, a comma, an exclamation, or an interrogation mark. Those who have made mistakes will correct them for themselves.

The pupils will write their spelling on the back of their paper and will make the fair copy on the paper that is folded in squares.

PRAYERS

CHAPTER VII

Prayers

ARTICLE I

Daily Prayers That Are Said in School

At the opening of school in the morning at eight o'clock, as soon as the bell has ceased ringing, all will make the sign of the cross and then say *Veni Sancte Spiritus, etc.;* in the afternoon will be said *Venez Saint Esprit, etc.,** as is indicated in the Manual of Exercises of Piety of the Christian Schools. Before and after breakfast and lunch and during the entire school time—from half past eight o'clock until ten o'clock and from two o'clock until half past three in the afternoon—the prayers which are indicated in the same book will be said.

There will always be two or three pupils, one from each class, kneeling in some place in the school which has been chosen by the Brother Director or the Inspector and arranged for this purpose, who will recite the Rosary in turn. At each hour of the day some short prayers will be said. These will serve to call the teachers' attention to themselves and to the presence of God and to accustom the pupils to think of God from time to time and to offer Him all their actions, so as to draw upon them His blessing. At the beginning of each lesson, a few short Acts will be said to

* *Come Holy Spirit, etc.* a hymn containing about ninety words, said, as above indicated, in Latin in the mornings and in French in the afternoons.

111

ask of God the grace of studying well and learning well.

The morning prayers will be said at a quarter before eleven, if the pupils assist at Holy Mass during school; but if they do not do so until the end of school in the morning, the morning prayers will be said at ten o'clock.

In the afternoon, the evening prayers will be said at the end of school at half past four. During the winter, from the first school day in November to the end of January, they will be said at four o'clock.

ARTICLE II

MEDITATIONS AT MORNING PRAYERS AND EXAMINATION OF CONSCIENCE AT EVENING PRAYERS

There are five meditations in the morning prayers for the five school days of the week. All of them will be read every day, a short pause being made after each one. The pupil who is reciting the prayers, after having read all of these meditations, will repeat that one of them to which special attention is to be given that day. Then a pause of the duration of a *Miserere* * will be made, during which the teacher will make a little exhortation, suited to the capacity of his pupils, on the subject of this meditation.

All of these five meditations will be repeated thus in order and will serve, each one in turn, as the subject of an exhortation on each of the five school days in the week. There is also an examination of conscience in the evening prayers, which contains those sins which children most ordinarily commit. This examination is divided into four

* That is to say, the length of time required to recite the Fiftieth Psalm, which begins with this word.

PRAYERS

articles, and each article into five points. Only one of these articles will be read each day, and this same article will be read every day during the week. Thus the four articles will be read in four weeks.

Each teacher will explain to his class one of the points of the article which is being read during that week, and he will make known in detail to the pupils the sins which they are liable to commit, without ever deciding whether the sin is mortal or venial. He will, at the same time, seek to inspire horror of these sins and suggest the means of avoiding them.

ARTICLE III

PRAYERS SAID IN SCHOOL ON SPECIAL OCCASIONS

On all Saturdays and on the eves of the feasts of the Blessed Virgin, after evening prayers, the litany of the Blessed Virgin will be recited.

On the eve of Christmas, of the Epiphany, and of the Purification, at the end of evening prayers, the litany of the Holy Child Jesus will be recited.

On the eve of the Feast of the Circumcision will be recited the litany of the Holy Name of Jesus; and on the eve of the Feast of Saint Joseph, the litany of that saint.

All will be recited in the manner that is indicated in the Manual of Exercises of Piety of the Christian Schools.

During the octave of Corpus Christi and on the Monday and Tuesday before Lent, instead of the Rosary which should be said in school, the pupils will be sent two by two, one from each class, or three by three, if there are three classes, or in a greater number according to the number of classes, one group after another, to the nearest church where the Blessed Sacrament is exposed, to adore it; and they will always remain there kneeling for half an hour. However, care will be taken that there be always one pupil capable of conducting the other or others.

On the three Ember Days, on the Feast of Saint Mark, and on the Rogation Days, in the morning after the prayer which is said on entering school and immediately before the prayer which is said before breakfast, the litany of the Saints will be recited; for the needs of the Church, for which it prays especially on these days, as well as for the priests and other ministers of the Church who are to be ordained on that Ember Saturday.

Whenever there is heard in the school the sound of the little bell which warns that the Blessed Sacrament is being carried to some ill person, all the pupils will kneel down, and each one of them in particular will adore the Blessed Sacrament until the teacher makes them a sign to rise.

When one of the teachers in the town dies, on the first three school days after his death, at the end of prayers, both in the morning and in the evening before the Benediction, the psalm *De profundis, etc.* will be said for the repose of his soul, the Reciter of Prayers saying one versicle and the pupils saying the next one; and when this psalm is finished, the Reciter of Prayers will say the collect *Inclina Domine, etc.* In the same manner, in all the Houses of the Institute, on one day a *De profundis* with the collect *Inclina, etc.* will be said in school.

When a pupil of one of the classes in a school dies, the psalm *De profundis* and the collect *Inclina Domine, etc.* will be said on the first school day after his death, at the end of evening prayers; provided the pupil be at least seven years old. No other prayers will be said in school, and on no other occasions than those which are indicated in the present article. Nothing will be added to it without the orders of the Brother Superior, who, in case of some public necessity or some other occasion which concerns the needs of the Institute, may have added, at the end of prayers, the litany of the Blessed Virgin or some other short prayer for a certain time only.

POSTURE OF THE TEACHER AND THE PUPILS DURING PRAYERS. MANNER OF SAYING THEM, AND THE ORDER THAT SHOULD BE MAINTAINED

The teacher will act during prayers, as well as on all other occasions, as he wishes the pupils to act. To this effect, during the prayers on entering school and the Acts which are said before going to Holy Mass, he will always remain standing before his chair, with a very serious demeanor, very restrained and thoroughly composed, his arms crossed and with great decorum, so as to give an example to the pupils of what they should do during this time.

The pupils will always kneel in regular rows, their bodies erect, their arms crossed, and their eyes lowered. The teacher will be careful that they do not move, that they do not change their position, that they lean neither on the bench before them nor on the one behind them, that they do not touch them nor seat themselves on their heels, that they do not turn their heads to look around them, and, above all, that they do not touch one another, which they will not do if the teacher sees that they always keep their arms crossed.

During the other prayers which are said at different times in school, the teacher and the pupils will remain seated at their places, the arms crossed and with the same decorous demeanor as it is indicated above that they should maintain at morning and evening prayers.

There will be in each school one student of the principal class who will be appointed to begin all the prayers which are said in school. For this reason, he will be called the Reciter of Prayers.

He will say alone all the titles of the Acts, the meditations, and the examination, all according to the usage established in the schools.

He will be especially careful to say the prayers in a tone and a manner intelligible to all and very slowly, so that the others can hear very distinctly all that he says even to the least syllable, and he will observe all the pauses. In the meanwhile, the teachers will see that the pupils do not cry out and that they do not speak too loud, but so that they can just be heard.

All the pupils will follow the Reciter of Prayers in such a manner that they will not say a single word either before or after he does. They will stop with him, and as long as he does, at all the pauses which he makes, so that there may be no confusion. The pupils will get ready to say the prayers as soon as the bell begins to ring, and the Reciter of Prayers will begin as soon as it has stopped ringing.

All will make the sign of the cross every time that the words *In nomine Patris, etc.* or *Au nom du Père, du Fils, etc.* are said and in the Benediction at the words Father, Son, and Holy Ghost.

The teacher will not speak to the pupils, neither to any particular one nor to them all in general, during prayers, either to reprimand them or for any other reason; nor will he correct any pupil during this time, for whatsoever reason it may be. If he notices some one of them who is doing something reprehensible and who deserves chastisement, he will defer it to another time. He will likewise abstain from everything that could attract the attention of the pupils which they owe to the prayers and from everything that might cause them distraction, such as to make a pupil pass from one place to another, etc.

The principal care of the teacher during prayers will be to watch with very great care over all that takes place in the school. He will also watch over himself, and much more during this time than at any other, so that he may not do anything ill timed and above all that he may not be guilty of any frivolity.

CHAPTER VIII

HOLY MASS

It will be so arranged everywhere that the pupils assist at Holy Mass in the nearest church and at the most convenient hour.

The most convenient time to go to Holy Mass is at the end of school in the morning. In order to go at this time, it will be necessary that the Mass should not begin before half past ten or thereabouts, so that, before going, there may be time to say the morning prayers, beginning them at ten o'clock.

If it is not possible to go to Holy Mass at the end of morning school, it will be arranged to go at or around nine o'clock.

ARTICLE I

Manner in Which the Pupils Should Leave School to Go to Holy Mass, and How They Should Deport Themselves on the Street When on the Way

When the pupils are made to go to Holy Mass at the end of morning school, they will prepare to leave the school in the same manner as in the afternoon at the end of school and as is indicated in the tenth chapter, which treats of leaving the school.

When they are made to assist at Holy Mass during school time, they will leave school in the order of the benches. The first one on a bench will take the second one as his companion, the third one will take the fourth one, and so on with the others. The teacher will take care that they all leave the school in silence, with great decorum and reserve, and that, while on the street on their way to the church, they walk two by two in a line. None should leave his companion or separate himself from him from the time they leave the school until they are kneeling in the church.

The teacher will take care that they do not go too near the walls, the shops, or the gutter and that they walk immediately behind the ones who precede them, only two paces distant from them. He will also take care that they walk sedately, without making any noise. He will urge them to say in a low tone, each one with his companion, the Rosary or some other prayers, so that they will be more attentive to themselves, more restrained, and more modest.

The teacher will watch very carefully over the pupils at this time. It would, however, be well that the pupils should not be aware of this.

He himself will give his pupils by his modesty and restraint an example of the manner in which they should walk. In order that he may more easily see his pupils and observe how they behave themselves on the way to Holy Mass, he will walk on the opposite side of the street from them, ahead of the ranks, with his face sufficiently turned toward his pupils to be able to see them all.

While on the street, he will not admonish his pupils for any faults of which they may be guilty, but will wait until the next day, just before going to Holy Mass.

Finally, he will take care from time to time to instruct the pupils in the school, while they are preparing to leave or while the pupils of the other classes are going out, concerning the manner in which they should walk on the street and behave themselves in the church and the edification which they are obliged to give their neighbor; and he will urge them thereto by Christian motives. He will also make them understand that he will be more careful to punish lack of restraint and the faults that they commit on the street and in the church than those which they commit in the school—this on account of the scandal which they would give those who might see them.

Manner of Entering the Church

The teacher will take the greatest care to have the pupils enter the church in silence and in a particularly proper manner.

It would be well that he should always enter the church before his pupils and that the teacher who follows him should be careful to watch over those of them who remain in the street as well as over his own. It is important that the teacher should watch carefully over the conduct of his pupils, especially when they are entering the church, in order to prevent them from making any noise, either with the tongue or with the feet, and to make them walk very modestly, with the eyes lowered, in the order that they should keep on the street, as is indicated above, and without the least confusion.

There will be one pupil, called the Aspergill Bearer, who will be charged with the duty of offering holy water to all the pupils, one after another as they enter or leave the church.

He will be the first to enter, and from time to time he will take holy water from the font with the aspergill, which he will hold in such a manner that all the pupils can easily touch it.

The teacher will not permit the pupils to take holy water directly from the font, and he will see that they take it from the aspergill in a proper manner which manifests the piety with which one should do this act. When the pupils reach the place in the church which is reserved for them, they will all kneel one after another.

The teacher will take care that the pupils be ranged in proper order in the church and that they be placed two by two, one pair behind another. Ordinarily they will be placed in several ranks of two each, depending upon the width and length of the place that they occupy. They will be ranged in such a manner that those in a same row or rank, both lengthwise and crosswise, will be exactly beside or behind one another in a straight line. If there are pillars in the middle of the place which they occupy, the pupils will be placed in such a manner that those of a same class will be between the pillars and the wall, in order that each teacher may be able to see his pupils easily and watch over them. They will be accustomed to range themselves without the teacher's being obliged to attend to them.

WHAT THE PUPILS SHOULD DO DURING HOLY MASS

The teacher of the lowest class in each school will see that the pupil who has charge of rosaries always brings them to church and that one be given to each pupil who does not know how to read. There will be as many of the best behaved pupils as there are ranks of two in the church who will be appointed to distribute the rosaries. As soon as the pupils are kneeling, the Keeper of Rosaries and his assistants will distribute them to each one in the rank which is assigned to him, going from the top of the rank to the bottom. They will collect them in the same manner at the end of Holy Mass, taking care to get them all and to lose none of them.

The teacher will take great care that all those who have rosaries use them to pray continuously and that they do not play with them. He will teach them in school, when they are being taught to say it, how to hold a rosary, and he will require them to hold it in such a way that it may be easily seen.

Each of those who know how to read will have a Manual of Prayers for Holy Mass arranged for the Christian Schools, and he will use it during this time.

In order to avoid the noise and confusion which it might occasion, pupils who assist all together at Holy Mass on school days will not rise when the priest reads the Gospels. The teacher will, however, recommend to them to make three times the sign of the cross at the beginning of each Gospel, at the response *Gloria tibi Domine:* the first on the forehead, the second on the mouth, and the third on the breast.

When the bell is rung to warn the faithful to prepare for the Consecration, all those who have books will place them under their arms, and those who have rosaries will put them on their arms. Then all will clasp their hands, as the teacher will also do, until after the Elevation. When the bell is rung for the Elevation, both of the Host and of the Chalice, all the pupils will bow their heads and bend slightly forward to adore Our Lord in the Host and His Precious Blood in the Chalice.

The Duties of the Teachers during Holy Mass

The teachers will keep a continuous watch over their pupils during Holy Mass, in order to observe the manner in which they behave, the faults that they may commit, and to prevent them from speaking with, or passing anything to, each other, from exchanging books, from pushing each other, or from doing any other of those foolish things which are only too common to children.

To prevent the pupils from falling into all these faults and into all the others which they could commit during Holy Mass, the three following means will be used: The first will be to oblige them to hold their books with both hands and not to cease reading them. The second will be that the teacher will place himself so that he can easily see the faces of his pupils. And the third will be to separate them always as much as possible from each other as the extent and arrangement of the place will permit.

The teachers will not leave their places to reprimand the pupils when they commit a fault, except in case of great necessity, nor will they threaten them in the church. They should be persuaded that it is not on their own account that they assist at Holy Mass when they take their pupils there, but only in order to watch over them. This is, therefore, the only thing of which they will think and will do then with attention. They will not have any books at this time, and they will content themselves with a simple application to the Sacrifice.

They will take care that the pupils bring into the church

nothing that is improper or that might be a subject of distraction, as their papers could be when they have finished writing them. If they bring a brazier during winter, they should put it in some place where it cannot be seen, and they should not make use of it when in the church.

What Must Be Done When Entering the Church after Mass Has Already Begun and Is Advanced

If Holy Mass has begun and is already advanced when the pupils reach the church, they will be made to assist at it, unless there is another beginning a little later. If there is another Mass which begins immediately after the one at which they arrived late, they will remain until the end of it; but if there is no other Mass following, they will remain in the church for as long a time altogether, including the time of the Mass at which they assisted in part, as it would take for an entire Mass.

Great care will be taken that the pupils all be in the church, ranged in order and kneeling, before the Mass begins. All necessary precautions to this effect will be taken, even though it be necessary to send a pupil to the church to give notice of their coming or to request that the bell be rung a little sooner or that the Mass begin a little later. This point is of very great importance, and, in case of necessity, it is better to omit the prayers rather than to fail to assist at Holy Mass.

When it is not possible to have the pupils assist at Holy

Mass on account of sleet or extraordinary rain, they will be made to say the Rosary in school. The pupils will stand, and a part of them will begin *Ave Maria, etc.,* and the others will continue *Sancta Maria, etc.*

How the Pupils Will Leave the Church

After Mass has ended, the pupils will remain in the church as long as it takes to say a *Pater Noster,* before returning to the school. The teacher or whosoever is in charge of the class that should be the first to leave will give the usual signal, at which all the pupils of a rank will rise, make a genuflection, and at once leave their places to go out two by two as they came. The same procedure will be followed for all the other ranks, and each teacher will do the same with his own class.

The pupils will return from the church to the school two by two, just as they went from the school to the church. The Brother Director or the Inspector of Schools or one of the teachers who has been charged with this duty will stand at the door of the church, to see that the pupils do not play or make any noise in the street and to take note of those who may do so or who may stop on the way. All the pupils will always walk two by two in the streets as well as in the church, at least four paces away from each other, in order to avoid noise and confusion. The teachers will take care to instruct the pupils concerning the manner of entering and of leaving the church.

CONDUCT OF THE SCHOOLS

ASSISTANCE AT THE PAROCHIAL MASS AND AT VESPERS

The pupils will be taken to the Parochial Mass when it can be easily done, and also to Vespers after Catechism on Sundays and holy days of obligation, in the nearest and most convenient church. It pertains to the Superior of the Institute to give orders concerning what should be done in this respect. The teachers will explain to their pupils the institution of the Parochial Mass and the manner of assisting at it, and if there is a sermon they will take care that they listen to it very attentively and respectfully. They will inspire them with a great respect and affection for the offices of the Church, especially for those which are celebrated in their own parishes. The pupils will, therefore, assemble in the church on Sundays and holy days of obligation. They will be required to be there before the *Asperges,* or blessing with holy water, and to remain until the end of the Mass. If there are benches for them in the church, they will seat themselves upon them; and the teachers will take care that they are in proper order. They will sit, stand, or kneel according to the usage of the diocese or the parish.

They will, however, all kneel during the Offertory and until the Preface, if there is no Offering, or until the Offering, if there is one and it is made immediately after the Offertory, in order to unite themselves during this action with the intention of the priest and to offer themselves also to God to be consecrated entirely to Him. They will stand throughout the Preface and will all kneel when the *Sanctus* is sung and remain kneeling until the end of the Mass.

If there are no benches for the pupils, they will stand all

the time that the others are seated, except during the Offertory. The teachers who are present to watch over them will see that they are always well ranged and in good order.

During the Parochial Mass and during Vespers, the teachers will always keep the pupils in sight and will take care that those who do not know how to read say the Rosary as on other days, and that those who know how to read have their Manual of Prayers for Holy Mass in their hands all the time at Mass, and an Office Book throughout Vespers, and that they read them continuously. When the pupils leave the church after the Parochial Mass and after Vespers, the same order will be observed as after Holy Mass on school days.

When the Blessed Bread * is given for the pupils, the one of them who has charge of the rosaries will bring a basket in which to put it, and at the end of the Mass he will distribute it to them all in turn.

CHAPTER IX

THE CATECHISM

ARTICLE I

TIME TO BE EMPLOYED IN TEACHING THE CATECHISM AND THE PARTS TO BE TAUGHT

The Catechism will be taught every day for half an hour, from four o'clock to half past four.

* In France, it is frequently the custom for different families in a parish to make in turn an offering of small loaves of bread or rolls, which are blessed at the High Mass and then distributed to the faithful present.

From the first day of November until the last of January inclusive, the Catechism will be taught from half past three until four o'clock.

On the Wednesdays preceding holidays, it will be taught for one hour, from half past three until half past four; in winter, from three o'clock until four. It will also be taught for one hour on the eves of the Feast of Saint Joseph, of the Presentation of the Blessed Virgin, of the Transfiguration of our Lord, and of the Exaltation of the Holy Cross. When there is a holy day in the week, there will be half holiday only on Tuesday or Thursday in the afternoon, and on that day in the morning the lessons will be shortened, and the Catechism will be taught for half an hour at the end of school. On Wednesday in Holy Week, in the afternoon, the pupils will neither read nor write, and only the Catechism will be taught from half past one until three o'clock, as is done on Sundays and holy days. The same will be done on the eves of the Feast of the Most Holy Trinity and of Christmas. At three o'clock, at the end of the Catechism, the prayers will be said, and the pupils will be dismissed in the regular manner.

On Wednesdays before whole holidays, on Sundays and ordinary holy days, the Catechism will be taught in all the classes. The first half hour will be spent on a summary of the principal Mysteries, and the rest of the time on the subject indicated for the week.

On solemn feasts, for which there is a particular subject in the Catechism, the subject of the feast or of the Mystery will be taught, as it is indicated in the Catechism.

The Catechism will be taught on the afternoon of Wednesday in Holy Week, from half past one until two o'clock on the principal Mysteries, and from two o'clock until three on the manner in which the ensuing days until Easter Sunday should be spent. On the eves of the Most Holy Trinity and of Christmas, the same will be done. On Mondays, the subject that will be treated throughout the week will be begun; and on Sunday—the last day on which this subject is treated—a summary will be made of all that has been propounded during the five days of the week. The teacher will also examine the pupils on all the questions contained in the lessons for the preceding five days, in those classes in which only the abridgment of Christian Doctrine is taught. On Sundays and holy days and on Wednesdays before a whole holiday, the Catechism lesson will be on the particular subject assigned for the week.

ARTICLE II

Manner of Asking Questions on the Catechism

The teacher will not speak to the pupils during Catechism as though he were preaching, but he will ask them almost continuously questions and subquestions. In order to make them understand what he is teaching them, he will ask several pupils, one after another, the same question. Sometimes he will ask it of seven or eight (or even of ten or twelve, and sometimes even of a greater number). He will question the pupils according to the order of the benches. If, however, he remarks that several, one after another, cannot answer the question or do not do so well, he may call upon one or several out of the regular order and in different parts of the class. Then, after having struck the signal once, he will make a sign to one to answer; and after one or several have answered, he will make the one answer upon whom he had called before in the regular order. He will question all his pupils each day—several times, even, if he is able to do so. However, from time to time he will interrupt the regular order and the sequence to question those whom he has observed to be inattentive, or even the more ignorant. He will be especially careful to question, and much more often than the others, those whose minds are slow and dull and who have difficulty in remembering, particularly on the abridgment of Christian Doctrine, and even more so on those questions in it which every Christian is obliged to know.

On the days of the week upon which the Catechism lesson is given for half an hour on the summary of the principal Mysteries, on Wednesdays or on Sundays and holy days, the teacher will not question the pupils on the summary in succession according to the order in which they are seated on the benches, as he does for the lessons on the subject assigned for the week, nor will he ask the questions in succession in the order in which they are in the Catechism; but he will sometimes question one or more in different places; and in the same way he will sometimes ask one or more questions on the Mysteries, sometimes one or more on the Sacrament of Penance, then on the Holy Eucharist or some other subject, and in the same manner without regular order for the others. He will continue to ask questions in this manner on the summary throughout the first half hour. In his questions, he will make use of only the simplest expressions and words which are very easily understood and which need no explanation, if this is possible, and he will make his questions as short as he can.

He will never permit an answer to be given word by word, but will require that the entire answers be given in sequence. If it should happen that some little child or some ignorant one is unable to give an entire answer, he will divide the question in such a way that the pupil may give in three answers what he had not been able to give in one.

If it even happens that some pupil has so slow a mind that he cannot repeat properly an answer that several others have given one after another, in order to make him retain it the teacher will have it repeated four or five times alternatively by a pupil who knows it well and by the one who does not know it, so as to afford him a greater facility for learning it.

ARTICLE III

DUTIES OF THE TEACHER DURING CATECHISM

One of the principal tasks of the teacher during Catechism is to conduct the lessons in such a manner that all the pupils will be very attentive and may easily retain all he says to them. To this effect, he will always keep all his pupils in sight and will observe everything they do. He will take care to talk very little and to ask a great many questions.

He will speak only on the subject assigned for the day, and he will guard himself against departing from his subject. He will always speak in a serious manner, such as will inspire the pupils with respect and restraint, and he will never say anything that might cause laughter. He will be careful not to speak in an indolent manner which could produce weariness. He will not fail to indicate in every lesson some practices to the pupils, and to instruct them as thoroughly as it is possible for him to do concerning those things which pertain to morals and to conduct which should be observed in order to live as a true Christian. But he will reduce these practices and these matters of morals to questions and answers, which will make the pupils very much more attentive and make them retain them more easily. He will take care not to disturb the Catechism lesson by untimely reprimands and corrections; and if it happens that some pupils deserve punishment, he will postpone it ordinarily until the next day, just before the Catechism, without letting them know it. He may, however, sometimes, but rarely, when he considers it unavoidable, give a few blows of the ferule during this time.

On Sundays and holy days, when the Catechism lasts three times as long as on the other days, he will always choose some story that the pupils will enjoy and tell it to them in a way that will please them and renew their attention. He will tell it with details that will prevent them from being bored. He will say nothing during the Catechism lessons that he has not read in some well-approved book and of which he is not very certain; he will never decide whether a sin is venial or mortal.

He may only say, when he judges such to be the case: "That will offend God very much." "It is a sin very much to be feared." "It is a sin that has evil consequences." "It is a grievous sin." Although sins should not be considered more grievous than they are, it is, however, more dangerous to make them appear slight and trifling. A great horror of sins, however slight they may appear, must always be inspired; an offense against God cannot be slight, and nothing that concerns Him can be trifling.

He will take care that the questions, the subquestions, and the answers to the subquestions fulfill the following four conditions: 1. They must be short. 2. They must make complete sense. 3. They must be accurate. 4. The answers must not be suited to the capacity of the most able and most intelligent pupils, but to that of the average ones, so that the majority may be able to answer the questions that are asked them.

The teachers will be so careful of the instruction of all their pupils that they will not leave a single one in ignorance, at least of those things which a Christian is obliged to know, in reference both to doctrine and to practice. In order not to neglect a matter of such great importance, they should often consider attentively that they will render account to God and that they will be guilty in His sight of the ignorance of the children who have been under their care and of the sins into which this ignorance has led them, if they who have been in charge of them have not applied themselves with sufficient care to deliver them from their ignorance, and that there will be nothing on which God will examine them, and by which He will judge them, more severely than on this point.

The teachers will help the pupils to acquire a perfect application to the Catechism. This is not naturally easy for them and is ordinarily of very short duration. For this purpose, they will employ the following means: 1. They will take care not to rebuff or to confuse them, either by words or in any other manner, when they are unable to answer properly the question which has been asked them. 2. They will encourage and even help them to say what they have difficulty in recalling. 3. They will offer rewards, which they will give from time to time to those who have been the best behaved and the most attentive—sometimes even to the more ignorant who have made the greatest effort to learn well. They will employ various other similar means, which prudence and charity will enable them to find, to encourage the pupils to learn the Catechism more readily and to retain it more easily.

ARTICLE IV

DUTIES OF THE PUPILS DURING CATECHISM

During the time when the Catechism is being taught, the pupils will be seated, their bodies erect, their faces and eyes turned toward the teacher, their arms crossed, and their feet in order. The teacher will make a sign with his signal to the first whom he wishes to question. The latter, before answering, will rise and uncover, then make the sign of the cross, removing his gloves if he is wearing them, and, having crossed his arms, will answer the question which has been asked him in such a manner that, by including the question, the answer will make complete sense.

When the first pupil has almost finished his answer, the one who comes next will rise, make the sign of the cross, saying the words in a tone low enough not to interrupt the one who is reciting, taking care to have made the sign of the cross by the time the other one has finished, and repeat the same answer, unless the teacher should ask him another question. All the others who follow on the same bench or on the next bench will do the same.

If the teacher should happen to call upon one or several pupils in succession out of the regular order, he whose turn it is to answer will remain standing during this time, until he is notified to speak. He will also remain standing if the other says something by way of explanation, and will answer as soon as the latter has finished speaking. A pupil, when answering during Catechism, will keep his eyes modestly lowered and will not stare fixedly at the teacher nor yet turn his head slightly to one side. He will keep his body erect and both feet properly placed on the floor. He will speak in a moderate tone but rather low than loud, so that, if possible, he will not be heard by the other classes and the other pupils will be more attentive. He will, above all, speak very slowly and distinctly, so that not only the words but also all the syllables may be heard. The teacher will see that he pronounces them all, particularly the last ones.

All the pupils will be very attentive during the entire Catechism lesson. The teacher will take care that they do not cross their legs and that they do not put their hands under their garments, in order that they may not do the least thing contrary to good behavior. He will not permit any pupil to laugh when another has not answered properly or any one of them to prompt another who is unable to answer a question. He will take care that the pupils go out of the room the least possible number of times during Catechism and only in case of great necessity.

CONDUCT OF THE SCHOOLS

PARTICULAR DETAILS CONCERNING CATECHISM FOR SUNDAYS AND HOLY DAYS

On all Sundays and holy days, there will be Catechism for an hour and a half, except on Easter Sunday, Pentecost Sunday, Trinity Sunday, and Christmas Day, when there will not be any. The pupils will assemble during the half hour preceding the time for Catechism; and while they are assembling, they will question one another, in groups of two, on the Diocesan Catechism, just as is done during breakfast and lunch. The teacher will indicate those who are to question one another and repeat the Catechism at this time.

In places where Vespers are sung at three o'clock, the Catechism will be recited from one o'clock until half past two, and the pupils will assemble between half past twelve and one o'clock. At half past two, they will say the prayers which are ordinarily said every day at the end of school in the afternoon; and after that, if there remains sufficient time, some verses of a canticle will be sung as usual. Then the pupils will be taken to Vespers.

In places where Vespers are sung at half past two o'clock, the Catechism will begin at half past twelve and will be finished by two o'clock. At two o'clock, the prayers will be said, and the pupils will be taken to the church as indicated above.

In places where Vespers are sung at two o'clock, at half past twelve the Catechism will be on the summary, and from one o'clock to two, on one special subject; the prayers will not be said. At two o'clock, the pupils will be taken to the church for Vespers, after which they will be sent home.

During the first half hour, the Catechism will be on the abridgment, and the teacher will do nothing but ask questions, without giving any explanations. He will not speak on one subject only, but will ask various questions on the abridgment, without following any regular order. During the next hour, the Catechism will be on the entire subject which has been taken in parts on each of the days of the preceding week, or on the subject of the feast. During this time, the teacher will question all the pupils several times, and at the end he will give some practical applications, which should be the fruits that they ought to obtain from the subject which he has expounded to them. Pupils who do not regularly attend the school may be admitted to the Catechism, provided they cause no disorder.

CHAPTER X

DISMISSAL OF SCHOOL

ARTICLE I

MANNER IN WHICH THE PUPILS SHOULD LEAVE THE SCHOOL

The pupils of the lower classes will leave the school before those of the higher ones. For example, those of the lowest class will be the first to leave, those of the next to the lowest will follow them, and so on for the other classes up to the highest. When there are three or more classes in the school of a neighborhood, the pupils of the lowest class will leave while the canticles are being sung. They will leave their classroom and the school two by two, each one with the companion that has been assigned to him.

The pupils will leave their classrooms in order and in the following manner: When the teacher makes a sign to the first pupil on a bench to rise, this pupil will leave his place, his hat off and his arms crossed, with the one who has been assigned to him as a companion. They will both stand in the middle of the classroom, side by side, and, after having made an inclination before the crucifix, they will turn toward the teacher to salute him. If the Brother Director, the Inspector of Schools, or some strangers happen to be in the classroom at this time, they will salute them first and then their teacher; after this they will go out decorously, keeping their arms crossed and their hats off until they are outside the classrooms.

When the first two pupils reach the middle of the room, the next in order on the same bench as the first who has been notified will rise with the one following him; they will likewise go to the middle of the room and will then make their inclination like the two others.

All the pupils of every class will go out in the same order and in the same manner. The teachers will see that they always walk two by two, at least a rod behind each other, until they reach their homes.

ARTICLE II

PRAYERS TO BE SAID BY THE PUPILS WHILE LEAVING CLASSES

As soon as the singing of the canticles is finished, the *Pater Noster*, the *Ave Maria*, the *Credo*, the *De profundis*,

138

and the *Miserere* will be recited aloud. The Reciter of Prayers will say alone in a loud and distinct tone: "Let us pray for our living benefactors, that God may preserve them in the faith of the Holy Catholic, Apostolic, Roman Church and in His Holy Love, and let us say *Pater Noster, etc.*" The other pupils will then continue to recite with him in a lower tone until the end of the Creed.

After the Creed has been recited, the Reciter of Prayers will say: "Let us pray for our benefactors who are dead, and let us say for the repose of their souls *De profundis, Requiem æternam, A porta inferi,* and *Domine exaudi, etc.*" All these prayers will be said alternatively in the manner that is usual in the school, and then the same Reciter of Prayers will say: "*Oremus. Fidelium Deus, etc.*," and the others will reply "*Amen.*"

When these prayers are finished, the Reciter of Prayers will continue to say alone in a loud voice: "Let us pray God to forgive us the faults which we have committed in school today, and let us say for that intention *Miserere mei Deus, etc.*" This psalm will be said alternatively like the psalm *De profundis.* The Reciter of Prayers will say one entire versicle, and all the pupils will say together the following one.

When the pupils have left the classroom, they will cease to pray aloud and will walk in silence and in order, following each other.

The teachers will, however, exhort their pupils, and will take measures to compel them, to walk with much restraint and decorum from the school to their homes. They will also urge them to recite the Rosary, each one with his companion, for the entire way, which will keep them in restraint and will, without doubt, be most edifying.

DUTIES OF THE TEACHERS WHILE THE PUPILS ARE LEAVING THE SCHOOL AND AFTER THEY HAVE LEFT IT

One of the teachers, if there are more than two, will look after the exit of the pupils from the last of the classrooms as far as the street door, attending at the same time to what takes place in that classroom. If there are only two teachers, one of them will watch over both classrooms, so as to make the pupils go out in order, and the other will watch the street door. The one to whom this duty has been assigned by the Brother Director will, therefore, be at the street door, and he will make sure that the pupils leave the school with order and restraint. He will see that the companions do not leave each other and, when the pupils are in the street, that they do not throw stones or cry out, that they do not approach too near to each other, and that they disturb no one.

The teachers will recommend particularly to their pupils not to satisfy their natural necessities in the streets, as this is a thing contrary to decency and modesty. They will admonish them to go for that purpose to places where they cannot be seen.

As the teacher cannot see what takes place except in the street where the school is situated, the Brother Director or the Inspector of Schools, jointly with the teachers, will direct some of the pupils to observe what occurs in the neighboring streets, above all where there are many pupils, and to report faithfully what they have observed.

However, these pupils must merely observe, without saying a single word; otherwise they should be punished, or some penance should be imposed upon them for having spoken.

When the last two pupils have left the school and have reached the street door and saluted the Brother Inspector or the teacher who is there, one of them will make a sign to him with the hand that there are no more pupils and that he may go in; thereupon, he will at once enter the school. When all the teachers are assembled in one of the classrooms and kneeling before the crucifix, if the school is in the house where the Brothers live, the Brother Inspector or the Head Teacher will say: "May Jesus live in our hearts," and the others will answer: "Forever." They will then all go to the living quarters. If, however, the school is at a distance from the Brothers' House, he will say: *"Dignare me laudare te, etc.,"* and the others will answer: *"Da mihi virtutem, etc.";* after this, the *Pater Noster* will be said, and then they will all leave the school in silence, continuing to say the Rosary all the way to the House. When they have arrived there, they will go to the oratory and will say the prayer *O Domina mea, etc.,* and after that: "May Jesus live in our hearts forever."

END OF THE FIRST PART

THE JUST MAN
LIVES BY FAITH

CONDUCT OF THE CHRISTIAN SCHOOLS

SECOND PART

MEANS OF ESTABLISHING AND MAINTAINING ORDER IN THE SCHOOLS

THERE are nine principal things that contribute to establishing and maintaining order in the schools: 1. The vigilance of the teachers. 2. The signals. 3. The registers. 4. The assiduity of the pupils and their exactitude in arriving on time. 5. The regulation of holidays. 6. The rewards. 7. The punishments. 8. The appointment of several officials and their faithfulness in fulfilling their duties. 9. The structure, quality, and uniformity of school buildings and suitable furniture.

CHAPTER I

VIGILANCE OF THE TEACHER IN SCHOOL

The vigilance of the teacher in school consists particularly of three things: 1. Correcting all the words which are mispronounced by a pupil when reading. 2. Making all the other pupils who have the same lesson follow when any one of them is reciting. 3. Enforcing a very strict silence. He should constantly pay attention to these three things.

CARE WHICH A TEACHER SHOULD TAKE IN CORRECTING WORDS, AND THE PROPER MANNER OF DOING IT

The teacher must be very exact in correcting all the words, syllables, and letters which a pupil pronounces badly when he is reciting his lesson. He must be convinced that the pupils will advance just so much the more rapidly in reading as he is exact on this point.

The teacher will not say a word or make any movement of the lips when making corrections in reading, but will strike the signal twice in rapid succession, and at once the pupil who is reading will repeat the last word which he has said. If he again pronounces incorrectly or it is not the word that he has mispronounced, the teacher will continue to strike the signal in the same manner until the pupil pronounces correctly the word that he has mispronounced. If he continues to say the word three times without perceiving the error that he has made or without correcting it, the teacher will make a sign to another pupil to correct him. This pupil will say only the letter, the syllable, or the word which the other has said incorrectly and which the latter will now repeat two or three times.

When a pupil fails in his lesson, the teacher must be exact in striking the signal at the very moment that he fails, so that he may not be obliged to look for the word that he has mispronounced. If, nevertheless, he fails on a word and continues to read two or three words before being stopped by the signal—for instance, if in reading *Seigneur Dieu tout puissant et éternel,* he should fail on the first syllable—care must be taken not to let him continue without correction; but on this occasion and on all others the signal must be repeatedly struck twice in succession until the pupil finds the word that he has mispronounced. Or else, the teacher will strike three times at first to indicate that the word at which he strikes the signal is not the one that has been mispronounced. If a pupil who is reading by syllables fails to pronounce properly and cannot correct himself, a sign must be given to some other pupil to correct him, which he will do not only by saying the syllable which the other has said incorrectly, but by repeating the entire word, pronouncing each syllable one after another. For example, if the reader, instead of saying *semblable,* should say *semblabe,* the pupil who corrects him will say *semblable* and not alone the syllable *ble.* The teacher will take great care that the pupils who are spelling do not draw out their syllables and that they do not repeat a syllable several times. If they do this, he will enjoin some penance, so that they may not accustom themselves to this manner of reading, which is very disagreeable and very difficult to correct once it is acquired.

He will likewise take care that the pupils do not pronounce too rapidly, clipping their syllables, for example, saying *qo;* he will see that they sound all the letters: *q, u, o.* He will also take care that they do not pronounce too slowly or drawl—which is very disagreeable—but that they pronounce evenly. When they read too rapidly or heedlessly, they are liable to put the following letter before the pre-ceding one, saying, for instance, *mo* for *om* or *su* for *us*. Furthermore, those for whom the lesson is new and those who are backward are unable to follow pupils who read too rapidly. Besides, pupils who read slowly and carefully learn much more readily.

Finally, he should take great care that a pupil who is reading pronounce so distinctly that all the others can easily understand; and that those who read with pauses read correctly, without drawling or acquiring any other un-becoming manner; that they pronounce all the syllables separately, so that they can be distinguished from each other; that they stop at all the pauses as much as is re-quired—a short pause at a comma, a slightly longer one at a semicolon, once again as long at a colon as at a comma, and once again as long at a period as at a colon.

ARTICLE II

CARE WHICH THE TEACHER SHOULD TAKE TO MAKE ALL THE PUPILS HAVING THE SAME LESSON FOLLOW IT

During all the lesson on the alphabet and syllable charts, in the primer and in the other books, both French and Latin, and even during the lessons in arithmetic, while one pupil is reading, all the others having the same lesson will follow; that is to say, they will read silently in their own books, without making any sound whatsoever with their lips, that which is being read by the one reading aloud.

The teacher will take care that all the pupils having the same lesson follow the one who is reading, syllable by syllable or word by word. Another pupil, when called to read, should continue without repeating any of the words that have been said by the preceding one. This will show better than anything else whether he has been following exactly.

The teacher will never permit the pupils to suggest to each other any letters, syllables, or words in the lessons, or even entire or partial answers, both during instructions and during catechizing. He will be very attentive to the lessons, and he will always keep his book in his hands, without, however, losing sight of his pupils, so that he may see if they are all following. In order that nothing may prevent him from being exact in this practice, he will hold nothing in his hands throughout the entire school time, except the signal and the lesson book—and pens, paper, and other things necessary for writing, if he is in charge of a class of writers.

If one of the pupils should play with anything in school, the teacher will order another pupil from among the most reliable to take it and keep it until the end of school. At that time, when all the others have left, he will return it to him, unless the teacher considers that it would be harmful for him.

The same thing will be done with books, printed sheets, or pictures which the pupils may bring to school, other than those which they need when they are there. The teacher will neither keep them nor read them during school time, even though he should believe it necessary to examine them in order to see if there be anything bad in them. He will do this at a moment at the end of school, when all the pupils have left, by looking at the title of the book.

The teachers will be exact in receiving nothing from the

pupils and in keeping nothing which they have brought to school, under any pretext whatsoever, except bad books, which they will take to the Brother Director, so that he may burn them. This point is of great importance.

A very useful means of obliging the pupils to follow the recitations is to observe the following practices: The first is to watch them constantly and very carefully, particularly those who are not exact in following. The second is to make each one of them read several times, a little each time. The third is to oblige all who are discovered not to be following to come of their own accord to receive the punishment for their fault and, in order to incite them to be faithful, to pardon them sometimes—above all, those who usually follow—and if they do not then do so, to punish them severely.

ARTICLE III

Care Which the Teacher Must Take to Enforce Silence in School

Silence is one of the principal means of establishing and maintaining order in schools. For this reason, every teacher will see that it is rigorously kept in his classroom and will permit no one to speak without permission.

To this effect, he will make the pupils understand that they must keep silent, not because he is present but because God sees them and it is His Holy Will.

He will keep a strict watch over himself, so that he may speak only very rarely and in a very low tone—unless it be necessary that all the pupils should hear what he has to say. He will always use a moderate tone when he gives them any instructions, as well as on all other occasions when he has need of speaking to all the pupils together. He will never speak, either to any pupil in particular or to all in general, until he has carefully thought about what he has to say and considers it necessary.

When he speaks, he will do so very seriously and in few words. When a pupil asks to speak to him, he will listen to him only very rarely and will not speak to him unless he himself is seated or is standing before his chair, and always in a low voice. He will not permit the pupils to speak or to leave their seats without permission during the time they are receiving some correction. He will make them understand that they are permitted to speak only three times in school: when reciting their lessons, during Catechism, and during prayers.

He will himself observe a similar rule, and will speak on only three occasions: 1. To correct the pupils during lessons, when necessary and when no pupil is able to do so. 2. During the Catechism. 3. During the Meditations and the Examination of Conscience. Except on these three occasions, he will not speak unless it seems to him to be necessary; and he will take care that this necessity be rare. When the pupils are moving about in the school, he will see that they are uncovered and have their arms crossed, that they walk very carefully, without dragging their feet or making any noise on the floor with them, in order that they may not disturb the silence which should be continuous in school.

To make it easy for the pupils to observe all these things, the teacher will take care that they be seated, always facing forward, with their faces turned slightly in his direction; that they always hold their books with both hands and that they always look at them; that they keep their arms and their hands placed in such a manner that he can always see them well; that they do not touch each other, either with their feet or with their hands; that they give nothing to each other; that they do not look at each other; that they do not speak to each other by signs; that they always have their feet properly placed and do not take them out of their shoes or sabots; and, finally, that the pupils of the writing class do not sprawl on the table or maintain any unseemly posture when reciting their lessons.

CHAPTER II

Signs Which Are Used in the Christian Schools

IT would be of little use for the teacher to apply himself to making the pupils keep silent, if he did not do so himself; and he will teach them this practice better by example than by words. His own silence will be more productive than anything else of very great order in the school, by giving him an opportunity to watch more easily over both himself and his pupils. However, as there are many occasions on which he is obliged to speak, a great many signs have been instituted in the Christian Schools; and, to make it easier for him to keep silence and to reduce these signs to some order, they have been classified according to those exercises and actions which most ordinarily occur in schools. Thus, to make the greater number of these signs, an iron instrument used in the Society and called the *signal* is employed.

All the signals used in all the Houses will be of the same form; nothing will be changed or added; and all the teachers will make use of the same signs. Those which are in use are explained in the following articles:

ARTICLE I

Signs Used during Meals

To have the prayers said, the teacher will clasp his hands.

To notify that the responses of Holy Mass are to be repeated, he will strike his breast.

To notify that the Catechism is to be recited, he will make the sign of the cross, or else he will indicate with the signal the place in the classroom where it is usually recited.

To discover whether a pupil is attentive during recitations, he will strike the signal once to stop the one who is speaking and will then point to the other pupil with the end of the signal, as a sign for him to repeat what his companion has just said.

ARTICLE II

Signs Concerning Lessons

To make a sign to the pupils to prepare to begin a lesson, the teacher will tap once with his hand on the closed book in which they are going to begin reading.

To make a sign to stop to a pupil who is reading, he will strike the signal once, and at the same time all the pupils will look. Then he will point to another one with the end of the signal, as a sign for him to begin.

To make a sign to a pupil who is reading to repeat when he has read badly or mispronounced a letter, a syllable, or a word, he will strike the signal twice in rapid succession. If, after he has made the sign two or three times, the pupil does not correct his mistake, the teacher will strike the signal once, as he does to make them cease reading, so that all the pupils will look at him. At the same time, he will make a sign to another pupil to read aloud the letter, the syllable, or the word which the former pupil has read badly or mispronounced. If, after the sign has been made two or three times, the pupil who is reading does not find and repeat the word which he has badly read or mispronounced—because he has read several words beyond it before being called to order—the teacher will strike three times in rapid succession, as a sign to him to begin to read further back; and he will continue to make this sign until the pupil finds the word which he has said incorrectly.

To make a sign to speak louder, the teacher will point upward with the end of the signal; and to make a sign to speak lower, he will point the end of the signal toward the ground.

To warn one or more pupils not to speak so loud when they are following the lesson or studying, he will slightly raise the hand in which he is holding the signal, as though he wished to carry it to his ear.

He will make the same sign when he hears any noise in

the school. If it is on his right that the noise is being made, he will raise his right hand; if it is on the left, he will raise his left hand.

To make a sign to read carefully, he will strike twice separately and distinctly.

To make a sign to spell a word which a pupil who is only beginning to learn to read does not say properly, he will place the end of the signal on the book which he has in hand.

To make a sign to a pupil who is spelling or reading by syllables, when he does not make a sufficiently long pause between two letters or between two syllables, he will slowly place the end of the signal several times on the book which he has in hand.

To make a sign to a pupil who is reading with pauses that he is not making a sufficiently long one at a comma, a colon, or a period, he will place the end of the signal on the passage that is being read and will hold it there.

To make a sign to a pupil who is reading, when he makes a pause where one should not be made or makes one that is too long; or to one who is spelling or reading by syllables, when he drawls in spelling or reading, the teacher will pass the signal over the open book.

To make a sign to change from one subject to another, he will strike the open book with his hand, and at once the pupil who is reading will say: "Blessed be God for ever and ever." All the pupils must remove their hats at once and make ready their books or lessons. All this should be done in an instant.

To make a sign to finish the last lesson and to put the books away, the teacher will strike twice with his hand on the book which he is holding and which is at that time being read.

SIGNS CONCERNING WRITING

To have the pupils begin writing after the papers have been distributed, the teacher will make three signs by striking the signal three separate times, once for each sign. At the first sign, the pupils will all take out their writing cases and place them in such a manner that they may all be in sight. At the second sign, they will open their writing cases, take out their pens and their penknives, if they have any, and will place them in the same manner. At the third sign, they will dip their pens in the ink and begin to write, all at the same time.

When a pupil sprawls on the table or assumes an unseemly posture when writing, the teacher will raise his hand from the right to the left, to make him a sign to place his body in a proper posture.

When one or more pupils do not hold their pens correctly, he will indicate with his hand how to do so; and if he notices someone who is not writing, he will make him a sign by looking at him; then he will raise his hand and move his fingers. If he again sees that the same pupil is not writing, he will inflict a penance on him.

SIGNS USED DURING CATECHISM AND PRAYERS

To make a sign to a pupil to cross his arms, the teacher will look fixedly at him, at the same time crossing his own arms; and to warn him to hold his body erect, he will look at him, then straighten his own body and arrange his feet.

When a pupil has not properly made the sign of the cross, the teacher will place his own hand on his forehead in order to make him begin again; and to make a sign to any pupil to lower his eyes, he will look at him fixedly, at the same time lowering his own eyes.

To make a sign to a pupil to clasp his hands, he will clasp his own hands while looking at him. In a word, on all these occasions and on all other similar ones, he will do while looking at the pupils what he wishes them to do or observe.

ARTICLE V

SIGNS USED IN REFERENCE TO CORRECTIONS

All the signs referring to corrections will be reduced to five, and the teachers will make the pupils understand for which of these five things they are to be punished.

The five things for which corrections will be inflicted in school are: 1. For not having studied. 2. For not having written. 3. For having been absent from school or for having come late. 4. For having been inattentive during Catechism. 5. For not having prayed to God.

These five things will be expressed by rules, which will be hung in various places in each classroom. Each of these rules will be expressed in the following terms:

1. A pupil must never be absent from school or come late without permission.

2. A pupil must apply himself in school to studying his lessons.

SIGNS

3. A pupil must always write without losing time.

4. A pupil must be attentive during Catechism.

5. A pupil must pray to God with piety in church and in school.

When a teacher wishes to correct a pupil, he will make him a sign to oblige him to look at him; and then he will show him with the signal the rule against which he has offended, at the same time making him a sign to approach. If it is to give him the ferule, he will make him a sign to extend his hand. If it is to give a correction, he will show him with the signal the place where it is received.

SIGNS THAT ARE USED ONLY ON SPECIAL OCCASIONS

When a pupil asks permission to speak, he will stand at his place, with his arms crossed and his eyes lowered, without making any sign. If the teacher permits him to speak, he will make him a sign to approach, by pointing the end of the signal toward himself. He will make use of the same sign every time that he has need of speaking to a pupil. If he refuses him permission to speak, he will point the signal toward the ground in his direction.

When a pupil asks permission to go to attend to the wants of nature, he will remain seated and will raise his hand. To grant this permission, the teacher will point the signal toward the door; and to refuse it, he will make him a sign to remain still, by pointing the signal toward the ground.

To make a pupil kneel, he will point with the signal to

the middle of the classroom; and to make one rise who is kneeling, he will raise his hand slightly while holding the signal.

CHAPTER III

Registers

One thing that can contribute much to the maintenance of order in the schools is that there be well-kept registers. There should be three kinds of registers: 1. The register of promotions to grades. 2. The register of sections of grades. 3. A pocket register.* The first of these will be for the use of the Inspector of Schools, and the last two will be used by the teachers.

ARTICLE I

Register of Promotions to Grades

The Inspectors of Schools will each have a register upon which the names of the pupils will be inscribed according to the grades and sections in which they are. The name of each pupil will be entered upon this register according to the section of a grade in which he is. There will be a separate register for each school controlled by the same House. Each register will begin with the first section of the lowest grade, continuing thus to the last section of the highest grade.†

* No further mention is made of this pocket register.
† See pp. 62 *f.* for the explanation of the terms used here.

The registers of pupils according to promotion to grades and in penmanship, both round hand and Italian, and in arithmetic will be written in the same book one after another.

Each leaf of this register will be divided into five columns, separated by lines from top to bottom. The middle column should be wider than the four others. All this will be arranged according to the following model:

MODEL

Register to be used for the Promotion to grades of Pupils of the School at . . . .

First line of Alphabet *

1	September		1	March
1	January		30	April
1	February		30	May
1	March		30	May
1	April		30	April
1	May		31	January
1	June		31	December
1	October		30	March
1	August		30	October
1	November		31	November
1	December		28	February
1	May			

In the middle column will be written the names and surnames of the pupils of the same section in a grade, one after another in the order in which they have been admitted to the school or promoted to this grade, as the

* See chart, p. 225.

case may be. In the first column, beside each name, will be written the day of the month that each of the pupils was put into this section of the grade. In the second column will be written the month. In the third column will be written the name and the surname. In the fourth column will be written the day of the month that each pupil of this section was transferred to another section. In the fifth column will be written the month in which the pupil was transferred.

REGISTER OF SECTIONS OF GRADES

Each teacher will have a register in the form of a book, containing twenty-four leaves, two for each month, upon which will be inscribed the names of the pupils of his class, according to the section of each grade in which they are. The names of all the pupils of a same section of a grade will be written, one after another, under the name of the section of the grade in which they are.

On each leaf of these registers there will be three columns which will be separated by lines from top to bottom. In the first column, which will be the narrowest, will be written, beside each name, the month and day of the month on which each of these pupils has been put into this section of the grade. In the middle column will be written the names and surnames of the pupils of the same section of a grade, one after another, in the order in which they have been admitted to the school or placed in the section of the grade in which they are. All the names will be separated from each other by lines drawn from one side of the sheet to the other. In the third column there will be four squares beside each name, in which will be marked by little dots as follows: in the first square, how many times a pupil has come late; in the second, how many times he has been absent with permission; in the third, how many times he has been absent without permission; in the fourth, how many times he has failed to know his lesson in the Diocesan Catechism. At the top of the first column of squares will be written *Late;* at the top of the second, *Ab. with p.;* at

MODEL

Register of the First Class of the School at............ for the Month of..............

Chart I *		Late	Abs. with p.	Abs. with-out p.	Ignor. of Cat.	Ill
Line I						
December 1.						
May 1.						
March 1.						
June 1.						
April 1.						
July 1.						
August 1.						

* See p. 225.

the top of the third, *Abs. without p.;* at the top of the fourth, *Ignor. of Cat.*

Toward the end of school, the teachers will mark on these registers those who have come late or been absent and those who have not known their Diocesan Catechism when called to recite it.

CHAPTER IV

REWARDS

From time to time, the teachers will give rewards to those of their pupils who are the most exact in fulfilling their duties, in order to incite them to do so with pleasure and to stimulate the others by the hope of the reward.

There are three kinds of rewards which will be given in the schools: First, rewards for piety. Second, rewards for ability. Third, rewards for assiduity.

The rewards for piety will always be more beautiful than the others, and the rewards for assiduity better than those for ability.

The things which may be given as rewards will be of three different degrees: First, books. Second, pictures on vellum, plaster statuettes, such as crucifixes and images of the Blessed Virgin. Third, pictures on paper, engraved texts, and even rosaries.

Engraved texts will most commonly be given to the pupils as rewards.

The pictures and texts will always be religious ones; and pictures of our Lord on the Cross, of the Mysteries, of the

Holy Child Jesus, of the Blessed Virgin, and of Saint Joseph will be used most ordinarily.

Rosaries, books, and other valuable objects of piety will be used only for extraordinary rewards and will be given only by the Brother Director, after he has examined those whom the teacher considers worthy to receive them.

The books which may be given as rewards will always be religious books, such as *The Imitation of Christ,* spiritual dialogues, Christian truths, thoughts and meditations, etc.

Only to poor children may be given hymn books, prayer books, Diocesan Catechisms, and other books that are used in the Christian Schools, and these will not be given to those who are able to buy them.

Rewards for ability will be given only once every month, after the Brother Director has examined the pupils. There will be but one for each grade. Every month, a reward may also be given to the pupil of an entire class who has excelled in everything, that is to say, to the one who has shown the most piety and decorum in church and, during prayers, the greatest ability and assiduity.

Every month, ten or twelve pictures, according to the discretion of the Brother Director, will be given to the teachers of each class, to be distributed by them to their pupils during the month.

CHAPTER V

Introductory Remarks on Corrections in General

The correction of the pupils is one of the most important things to be done in the schools and one with which the greatest care must be taken in order that it may be timely and beneficial, in respect to both those who receive it and those who witness it. For this reason, there are many things to be considered in regard to the use of the corrections which may be administered in the schools and which will be discussed in the following articles, after the necessity of joining gentleness to firmness in the guidance of children has been explained.

Experience, founded on the unvarying teachings of the saints and the examples which they have set us, affords sufficient proof that, to perfect those who are committed to our care, we must act toward them in a manner at the same time both gentle and firm. Many, however, are obliged to admit, or at least they show by the manner in which they behave toward those in their care, that they do not easily see how these two things can be joined together in practice. If complete authority and too much power, for example, are assumed in dealing with children, it appears difficult that this manner of controlling them (although it may proceed from great zeal, it is not according to knowledge, as Saint Paul says, since human weakness is so easily forgotten) should not become too harsh and unbearable.

On the other hand, if too much consideration is had for human weakness, and, under pretext of having compassion for them, children are allowed to do as they will, the result will be wayward, idle, and unruly pupils.

What, then, must be done in order that firmness may not degenerate into harshness, and gentleness into languor and weakness?

To throw some light on this matter—which appears

to be of no little importance—it seems opportune to set forth in a few words some principal points to which almost all the severity and harshness encountered in the manner of guiding and educating children may be reduced; and then some others from whence proceed, on the contrary, all laxness, disorder, etc.

Conditions that render the conduct of a teacher unbearable to those in his charge are:

First, when his penances are too rigorous and the yoke which he imposes upon them is too heavy. This state of affairs is frequently due to his lack of discretion and judgment; for it often happens that pupils have not enough strength of body or of mind to bear the burdens which many times overwhelm them.

Second, when he enjoins, commands, or exacts something of the children with words too harsh and in a manner too domineering; above all, when this arises from unrestrained movements of impatience or anger.

Third, when he urges too much upon a child the performance of something which he is not disposed to do and does not permit him the leisure or the time to reflect.

Fourth, when he exacts with the same ardor little things and big things alike.

Fifth, when he at once rejects the reasons and excuses of the children and is not willing to listen to them at all.

Sixth, finally, when, not considering himself, he does not know how to sympathize with the weaknesses of children, exaggerating too much their faults, and when he reprimands them or punishes them, acts as though he were dealing rather with an insensible instrument than with a creature capable of reason.

Conditions under which, on the contrary, the conduct of children becomes negligent and lax are:

First, when care is taken only about things that are important and which cause disorder and when others less important are imperceptibly neglected.

Second, when not enough insistence is placed upon the performance and observance of the school practices and those things which constitute the duties of the children.

Third, when what has been enjoined is easily permitted to be neglected.

Fourth, when, in order to preserve the friendship of the children, too much affection and tenderness are shown them, granting something special to the more intimate or giving them too much liberty, which does not edify the others and causes disorder.

Fifth, when, on account of natural timidity, the children are addressed or reprimanded so weakly or so coldly that they do not pay any attention, or it makes no impression upon them.

Sixth, finally, when the duty of a teacher in respect to his deportment—which consists principally in maintaining a gravity which keeps the children in respect and restraint—is easily forgotten, either by speaking to them too often and too familiarly or by doing some undignified act.

It is easy to recognize by all these things in what consist too much harshness and too much gentleness. Both of these extremes must be avoided, in order not to be too harsh or too weak, so as to be firm in attaining the end and gentle in the means of attaining it, and to show great charity accompanied by zeal. It is necessary to have great patience, without, however, permitting the children to aspire to impunity or to do what they wish, etc.; for in such matters there should be no gentleness. We must know that gentleness consists in never allowing any harshness or anything whatsoever that savors of anger or passion to appear in reprimands, but in showing therein the gravity of a father, a compassion full of tenderness, and a certain gentleness, which must be, however, lively and efficacious; and let it be made clearly to appear by the teacher who rebukes or punishes that it is a species of necessity and that it is out of zeal for the common good that he does so.

Different Kinds of Corrections

The faults of children can be corrected in several different manners: 1. By reprimands. 2. By penances. 3. By the ferule. 4. By the rod. 5. By expulsion from school. As there is something special to remark about penances, they will receive special consideration after all else pertaining to punishments has been discussed.

Section I

Reprimands

As one of the principal rules of the Brothers of the Christian Schools is to speak rarely in their schools, the use of reprimands ought to be very rare. It seems even much better not to make use of them at all. Threats may be used; but as they are of the same nature as reprimands, this must be done rarely and with much circumspection. When a teacher has threatened the pupils with something, and one of them commits the fault on account of which they have been threatened, he must be punished invariably—never pardoned.

Unconditional threats must never be made; for example: "You will get the ferule!" or "You will be punished!" Threats should always be subject to some condition, such as: "Anyone who fails to pray during Holy Mass or comes to school late will be punished."

Ordinarily, threats must be made by signs, as indicated in respect to signs pertaining to corrections.

A teacher may, nevertheless, sometimes speak to his pupils in a firm manner in order to intimidate them, without affectation, however, and without passion; for if it were with passion the pupils would easily notice it, and God would not grant His blessing.

Section II

Punishment with the Ferule: When It May and Should Be Used; the Manner of Using It

The ferule is an instrument consisting of two pieces of leather sewn together. It should be from ten to twelve inches in length, including the handle, and should terminate in an oval of two inches in diameter. The inside of this oval should be stuffed, so that it will not be completely flat but somewhat rounded on the outside.

The ferule may be used on several occasions: 1. For not having followed during a lesson or for having played. 2. For having come to school late. 3. For not having obeyed at the first sign; and for several other similar reasons, that is to say, for faults that are not very important.

Only one blow on the hand should be given with it;

and if it is sometimes necessary to give more, two should never be exceeded.

The left hand should be struck, especially in the case of pupils in the writing class, so as not to make the right hand heavy, which would be a great obstacle in writing.

It should not be given to those whose hands are sore, on whom should be imposed some penance; for it is necessary to foresee the accidents that might arise from this punishment and to try to avoid them.

The pupils should not be allowed to cry out when receiving the ferule or any other punishment. If they do so, they must be punished again without fail for having cried out and made to understand that it is for this that they are being punished.

It must be noted that when the ferule or any other punishment is given to a pupil for having committed some fault which caused him to neglect his duties, such as for having talked or played in school or in church or for having looked behind him, etc., he must not be told that it is for having talked or played, etc., but that it is for not having studied his lesson or for not having prayed in church.

Section III

Punishment with the Rod

According to the usage established in the Christian Schools, the rod may be used to punish the pupils: 1. For not having been willing to obey. 2. When they make a practice of not following the lessons and of not studying. 3. For having scribbled on their paper instead of writing. 4. For having fought in school or on the streets. 5. For not having prayed in church. 6. For not having behaved with decorum at Holy Mass or during Catechism. 7. For having been absent from school, from Mass or from Catechism on Sundays and holy days through their own fault.

This punishment should be administered with great moderation and presence of mind. Ordinarily, no more than three blows should be given; and if it is sometimes necessary to go beyond this number, never more than five should be given without a special order from the Brother Director.

Section IV

Expulsion of Pupils from School

Pupils may be, and sometimes ought to be, sent away from school; but this should be done only upon the advice of the Brother Director. Those who should be sent away are the dissolute, who are capable of ruining others; those who absent themselves easily and often from school, from the Parochial Mass or from Catechism on Sundays and holy days through the fault of their parents, and with whom it is becoming a habit; the incorrigible, that is to say, those who, after having been corrected a great number of times, do not amend their conduct. It should, however, be an extraordinary occurrence to send a pupil away from school.

ARTICLE II

FREQUENT PUNISHMENTS AND HOW TO AVOID THEM

If it is desired that a school be well regulated and in very good order, the punishments must be rare.

CORRECTIONS

The ferule must be used only when necessary, and things must be so ordered that this necessity be rare. It is not possible to determine precisely the number of times that it may be given each day, because of the different circumstances that may render it obligatory to use it more or less frequently. Nevertheless, it should be made possible not to exceed three times in a half day.

Punishment with the rod, etc., should be much rarer than with the ferule; it should be inflicted only three or four times in a month at most.

Extraordinary punishments should, consequently, be very rare for the same reason.

To avoid frequent punishments, which are a source of great disorder in a school, it is necessary to note well that it is silence, restraint, and watchfulness on the part of the teacher that establish and maintain good order in a class, and not harshness and blows. A constant effort must be made to act with skill and ingenuity in order to keep the pupils in order while making almost no use of punishments.

In order to succeed well, the same means must not always be used, inasmuch as the pupils accustom themselves to them. Rather is it necessary sometimes to threaten, sometimes to punish, sometimes to pardon and to make use of the various other means which the ingenuity of a skillful and thoughtful teacher will easily suggest to him on these occasions. If, however, a teacher should happen to think of some particular means which he believes would be adapted to keeping the pupils at their duties and forestall punishments, he will propose it to the Brother Director, and he will not make use of it until he has received the permission of the latter.

The teachers will not administer any extraordinary punishments without having first consulted with the Brother Director, and for this reason they will defer them, which is, at the same time, a very proper thing to do, in order to have adequate time for some reflection beforehand and to give more weight to the punishment; thus causing it to leave a greater impression on the minds of the pupils.

CONDITIONS UNDER WHICH PUNISHMENTS SHOULD BE ADMINISTERED

Punishment, in order to be beneficial to the pupils, should be accompanied by the ten following conditions:

First, it must be pure and disinterested, that is to say, purely for the glory of God and to fulfill His Holy Will, without any desire for personal vengeance, the teacher giving no thought to himself.

Second, it must be charitable; that is to say, it must be administered out of a motive of true charity toward the pupil who receives it and for the salvation of his soul.

Third, it must be just; and for this reason, it is necessary to examine carefully beforehand whether the matter for which the teacher is considering punishing the pupil is effectively a fault and if this fault deserves punishment.

Fourth, it must be proper and suitable to the fault for which it is administered; that is to say, it must be proportioned to the fault, both in nature and in degree. Just as there is a difference between faults committed through malice and obstinacy and those committed through weak-

ness, there should also be a difference between the chastisements with which they are punished.

Fifth, it must be moderate; that is to say, it should be
rather less than more rigorous, of a just medium; neither
should it be administered precipitously.

Sixth, it must be peaceable, so that he who administers
it should not be moved to anger, but should be entirely
master of himself, and he to whom it is administered should
receive it in a peaceable manner, with great tranquillity
of mind and outward restraint. It is even necessary that
he who inflicts a punishment should take great care that
nothing appear in his demeanor that might indicate that
he is angry. For this reason, it would be very proper to
defer a punishment until a time when one no longer feels
agitated, in order not to do anything that one might later
repent.

Seventh, it must be prudent on the part of the teacher,
who should pay great attention to what he does, so as to
do nothing inappropriate and that could have evil consequences.

Eighth, it must be voluntary and accepted on the part
of the pupil, every effort being made to make him consent
to it, by representing to him the magnitude of his fault
and the obligation under which he is to remedy it, the
great harm that he can do to himself and, by his bad example, to his companions.

Ninth, it must be respectful on the part of the pupil, who
should receive it with submission and respect, as he would
receive a chastisement with which God Himself would
punish him.

Tenth, it must be silent; in the first place on the part

of the teacher, who should not speak, at least not aloud, during this time; in the second, on the part of the pupil, who ought not to say a single word or cry out or make any noise whatsoever.

Faults Which Must Be Avoided in Punishments

There are many faults that must be avoided in punishments, and it is important that the teachers should pay very particular attention to them. The principal ones which must be avoided are the following:

No punishment should be administered unless it be considered useful and advantageous. Thus, it is bad to administer one without having previously considered whether or not it will be of some use, either to the pupil to whom it is to be administered or to the others who are to witness it.

When a punishment is considered useful only to give an example to the others and not to him who is to receive it, it should not be administered, unless it be necessary in order to maintain order in a class; and when it is possible to defer it, the advice of the Brother Director should be asked. If it is a case concerning a teacher of one of the lower classes, he will ask advice of the Head Teacher; and in case it concerns the Head Teacher, he will undertake it only with much precaution and under an evident necessity.

No punishment that could be harmful to him who is to receive it must ever be administered; for this would be to act directly contrary to the aim of punishments, which have been instituted only to do good.

CORRECTIONS

None should be administered that could cause any disorder in the class or even in the school, as would, for example, one that would serve only to make a child cry or to repel him, to embitter him, or to make him leave school, so that he would later hold the school in aversion, and the complaints that he or his parents would make could repel others and prevent children from coming. The teachers should endeavor to foresee these inconveniences before administering any punishment; for it is important not to incur them.

A pupil should never be punished on account of a feeling of aversion or of annoyance that one has for him, because he causes trouble, or because one has no liking for him. All these motives, which are either bad or merely human, are very far from those which should animate people who ought to act and conduct themselves only according to the spirit of faith.

Nor even should one be punished because of some displeasure caused by him or his parents; and if a pupil should happen to be lacking in respect for his teacher or to commit some fault against him, he should rather be urged by words to recognize his fault and correct it than punished for it. Even if it should be necessary to punish him on account of the bad example which he has given, it would be well to assign some other motive for the punishment, such as having caused disorder or having been obstinate.

When administering punishments, familiar forms of address must not be used: instead of *tu, toi, ton, va, viens*, one should say *vous, votre, vos, allez, venez*, etc.

It is also important never to use insulting words or words that are even in the slightest degree unseemly, such, for example, as rascal, knave, and sniveler. None of these words should ever be in the mouth of a Brother of the Christian Schools.

No punishments should ever be used other than those in use in the Christian Schools. Thus, pupils should never be slapped or kicked, nor should they be struck with the pointer; and it is altogether unworthy of the dignity and seriousness of a teacher to pull the children's noses, ears, or hair, even more so to strike or push them roughly or to pull them by the arms.

The ferule must not be thrown at a pupil for him to bring it back; that is highly unbecoming. A pupil must not be struck with the handle of the ferule on the head, on the back, or on the back of the hand; nor must two blows in succession be given with it on the same hand.

In using the ferule, great care must be taken not to strike either the head or the body—nowhere other than in the palm of the hand.

Great care must be taken in punishing a pupil not to strike him on any place where he may have any sore or ill, for fear of increasing it, and not to strike so hard that marks may appear.

A teacher should not leave his place to give the ferule or speak while giving it; and he should not allow the pupil who is receiving it to speak, much less to cry aloud, either when he is being punished or afterward.

He will also be careful not to assume any improper posture when administering punishment—as to stretch his arms or contort his body—or to make any other unseemly motions contrary to decorum.

He will, finally, be very exact in not administering any

punishment impulsively or when he is agitated; and he will watch so carefully over himself that neither angry passions nor the least touch of impatience shall have any part in his punishments; for that alone would be able to prevent the benefit and put an obstacle to the blessing that God would give.

Concerning who should or should not administer punishments, the usage will be thus: Every teacher may, in his own class, use the ferule as often as necessary. Brothers who have not yet attained the age of twenty-one will not administer punishments with the rod, etc., unless they have consulted the Brother Director, or him whom he has put in charge of such matters, and have taken his advice upon the subject. The Brother in charge of such matters will also watch very carefully over the punishments which these younger Brothers administer, either with the ferule or otherwise; and he will make a report twice each week to the Brother Director on all punishments that have been administered in the classes.

The same line of conduct will be followed, in respect to the Brothers who have attained the age of twenty-one, during the six months of trial which they will spend in the schools and during the first year after their novitiate.

ARTICLE V

Children Who Must or Must Not Be Punished

There are five vices which must not ordinarily be pardoned: 1. Lying. 2. Fighting. 3. Theft. 4. Impurity. 5. Indecorum in church.

Liars must be punished for their lies—even the least—

in order to make the pupils understand that there are no little lies in the sight of God, since the Devil is the father of lies, as Our Lord tells us in the Holy Gospel. Let them be pardoned rather, or punished less severely, when they frankly acknowledge their faults; they may be afterward made to conceive the horror which they ought to have of them, and they will be obliged to ask pardon humbly of God, kneeling in the middle of the classroom. Those who have been fighting will be punished in the same way. If it has been two or more of the pupils, they will be punished together. If it has been a pupil and another who is not of the school, the teacher will inform himself particularly concerning who was at fault, and he will not punish the pupil unless he is very certain that it was he. He will be very careful to act in the same manner in regard to all other faults committed outside the school. If it is a case of pupils who have been fighting in the school, they ought to be exemplarily punished, and they will be made to understand that this fault is one of the gravest that they can commit. Those who have taken and concealed anything, however small its value be, even if it be only a pen, will be similarly punished; and if they are found to be subject to this vice, they will be expelled from the school. The same punishment will be administered to those who have been guilty of any impure act or have used obscene words. Those who have been playing with persons of the opposite sex or who have been frequenting their society will be seriously warned the first time, and, if they persist in this fault, they will likewise be severely punished.

The teachers will often seek to instill into their pupils a great disinclination for the society of these persons and will urge them never to mingle with them; and even if they are their relatives, and they are sometimes obliged to converse with them, however small they be, let it be very rarely and always in the presence of their parents or of some sensible elderly persons.

Those who have been lacking in decorum in church will be severely punished, and they will be made to understand the great respect that they must have for God in this holy place and that it is to be lacking in faith to be there without piety and without both inner and outward restraint.

For this last fault, all kinds of pupils, large and small alike, must not be equally punished; for, unless the little ones are very carefully watched while they are in church, and unless the teacher has acquired great authority and control, it will be difficult for them to observe the decorum and restraint that is exacted of them. It is necessary, however, to pay great attention to this matter; and there is nothing that should not be done to prevent any pupil from behaving indecorously in church.

If any teacher is not himself sufficiently vigilant and does not possess sufficient authority to keep order in church, another teacher must be appointed to do so; let him do on this occasion what the other is unable to do.

Section I

Ill-bred and Wayward Children

There are some children to whose conduct their parents pay very little attention—sometimes none at all. From morning until evening, they do only what they please; they have no respect for their parents; they are disobedient; and they grumble at the least thing. Sometimes these faults do not come from an evil disposition of heart or mind, but from their having been left to themselves. Unless they are naturally of a bold and haughty temperament, they must be frequently admonished, but also punished in their bad humors; and when they let some of their faults appear in school, they must be subdued and rendered submissive. If they are of a bold and haughty spirit, they should be given some charge in the school, such as Inspector, if they are considered qualified, or Collector of Papers, and they should be promoted in something, such as writing, arithmetic, or spelling, in order to inspire them with liking for school. Moreover, they must be punished and mastered—never allowed, in whatsoever it be, to act as they please. If such pupils are small, there are fewer measures to be taken; they must be corrected while they are young, in order that they may not continue in their bad conduct.

As for those who are bold and insolent, one must speak with them little, and this always seriously. When they have committed some fault, they should be humbled and punished, if it appears that it would be useful to them to confuse and humble their spirit. They must be held in check and not suffered to reply to anything that is said to them. It would be well to admonish them and reprimand them sometimes in private for their faults, but always with great seriousness and in a manner which will keep them respectful.

As for those who are heedless and frivolous, they must be punished little, because ordinarily they reflect little, and a short time after having been punished they sometimes fall again into the same fault or into another which deserves the same punishment. Their faults do not come from pure malice but from thoughtlessness. They must be treated in such a manner as to prevent them from misbehaving, by showing them affection, without, however, giving them any charge. They should be seated as near the teacher as possible—under pretext of obliging them, and effectively in order to watch over them—and placed between two pupils of a sedate disposition who do not ordinarily commit faults. They should also be given some rewards from time to time, in order to render them assiduous and fond of school—for it is these who absent themselves the most frequently—and to induce them, while they are there, to remain still and silent.

Section II

Stubborn Pupils

The stubborn must always be corrected—above all, those who resist and are not willing to suffer correction. However, two precautions must always be taken in regard to this kind of children: 1. Not to attempt to punish them without having well examined the faults that they have committed, and unless it is clear that they deserve punishment. 2. When such a child resists, either because he does not wish to submit to punishment or because he does not want to leave his seat, it will then often be very much to the purpose to let his bad humor pass and, to this end, not to let it appear that there is any intention of correcting him. Some time later, the teacher will make him come to speak to him; he will gently make him realize and admit his

fault, both the original one and that of which he was guilty
in resisting, and then he will punish him exemplarily. In
case he is not yet willing to receive his punishment, he
must be forced to do so; for only one example of resistance
would be needed to produce several others afterward. Some
time after this pupil has been punished, when the teacher
thinks that his bad humor has passed, he will make him
draw near to him in order gently to make him reflect;
and he will make him afterward admit his fault and ask
pardon kneeling.

However, matters must be so ordered as to forestall this
sort of resistance and to make it happen very rarely; for
otherwise it would cause a very bad effect in a school.

There is another kind of stubborn children who mutter
after they have been punished and, when they have returned to their seats, lean their heads on their arms or
maintain some other unseemly posture. Such manners must
never be suffered, and these pupils should be obliged to
study or to follow the lesson. If the teacher cannot prevent
a pupil whom he has punished from grumbling, from
muttering, from weeping, or from disturbing the school
in some other manner, either because the pupil is very small
and has very little intelligence or for some other reason,
and it has been observed that punishments not only do
not bring him to his duty but perhaps even render him
more indocile, it would ordinarily be more to the purpose
not to correct him, but to pretend not to notice it when
he does not study or fails to do his duty in some other
thing, or even to send him away.

On such occasions, the teachers will take care to obtain
orders from the Brother Director concerning what they

should do. Silence during punishment and a correct manner of administering it will ordinarily prevent the greater number of these failures.

Section III

Children Who Have Been Gently Reared and Those of a Timid Disposition. Stupid and Sickly Children. Little Children and Newcomers

There are some parents whose manner of bringing up their children is to give them all that they ask; they never gainsay them in anything and almost never correct them for their faults. It seems that they fear to cause them pain, so they cannot suffer that the least correction be administered to them.

Such children are almost always of a gentle and peaceable nature, and, for that reason, it is ordinarily better not to punish them, but to correct their faults by some other means, such as giving them some penance that is easy to perform, by preventing their faults in some skillful manner, pretending not to see them, or by admonishing them gently in private.

If it is sometimes felt that it is necessary to punish them, it should not be done without consulting the Brother Director or the Head Teacher; and in such cases they should be little punished and very rarely.

If the means that are used to prevent their faults or to correct them are of no avail, it is often better to send them away than to punish them; unless it be after speaking with their parents and making them agree that it will be well to punish them.

As for those who have a gentle and timid disposition, they should not ordinarily be punished. The example of those who do well, the fear which they naturally have of the chastisements which they see inflicted, and some penances will suffice to make them do their duty. They do not often commit faults, and they easily keep still. Furthermore, their faults are not considerable, and they should sometimes be tolerated in them. At times, a warning will suffice for them; at others, a penance. Thus, there will be no need of having recourse to punishments and chastisements to keep them in good order.

Much the same can be done in the case of stupid children who make noise only when it becomes necessary to punish them. Ordinarily, it must not be done; and if they are troublesome in school, it is better to send them away. If they cause no trouble and create no disturbance, they should be let alone.

The ordinary faults of this kind of children are not to follow the lesson, not to read well, not to retain or recite well the Catechism, to learn nothing or very little. What is beyond their capacity must not be required of them. No more should teachers be discouraged by them; they should manage somehow to advance them, encourage them from time to time, and be satisfied with the little progress that they make.

In respect to those who are sickly, it is of importance that they should not be punished—above all, when the punishment might increase their ailment. Some other means of correction should be used with them, some penance imposed on them.

There are also many little children who likewise must

not be punished or who should be punished very seldom, because, not having attained the use of reason, they are not capable of profiting by punishment. It will be necessary to deal with them in much the same manner as with children of a gentle and timid disposition.

Finally, one must abstain from punishing children who are just beginning to come to school. It is necessary, first, to know their minds, their natures, and their inclinations. They should be told from time to time what they are to do; and they should be placed near some pupil who acquits himself well of his duties, in order that they may learn by practice and by example. They should ordinarily be left about a fortnight in school before being punished. Punishment of newcomers can only repel them and alienate them from school. But, if it is important to act thus in respect to new pupils, it is of no less importance for a teacher who is new in a class to refrain from administering any punishment until he knows his pupils.

Section IV

Accusers and Accused

The teachers will not easily listen to reports and accusations made against pupils; however, they will not rebuff those who make them but will be careful to examine them well and not to punish without due consideration, or immediately, for reports that have been made to them.

If it is some of the pupils who report or accuse one of their companions, the teacher will, at the very instant, inform himself privately whether other pupils have seen the fault committed, and he will manage in such a way as to learn some circumstances that will make him discover the truth. If the matter appears to him dubious or not altogether certain, he will not punish the accused, unless the latter himself admits his fault, and then he will punish him much less—only by assigning to him a penance, but making him understand that this is because he has told the truth. If he ascertains that the pupil has been falsely accused or that it is through revenge or some other passion that it has been done, the accuser will be severely punished.

If it is parents who come to accuse their children and say that they should be punished, the children should not be punished on this account; for parents often speak thus from anger, and they would not do so at any other time. If, however, the fault deserves punishment, the parents must be given to understand that they should punish their children themselves. If it happens that several pupils commit the same fault and each one knows that the others are guilty, all of them must be punished, as, for instance, in case several pupils have been fighting or two or three have been talking or playing during Holy Mass. However, if several have committed the same fault and they do not know each one that the others are guilty, or if they believe that the teacher is ignorant of it, it will ordinarily be well to punish only one of them and to pretend to be unaware of the faults of the others.

On such occasions, the pupil whose punishment will be of the greatest profit, both to himself and to the others, must be punished. Thus, on these occasions, those whom an example alone suffices to frighten and make attend to their duties and those who have committed a fault for the first time or who commit it rarely should not be punished.

CORRECTIONS

METHOD OF ADMINISTERING PUNISHMENTS

When the teacher wishes to give the ferule to a pupil, he will make the ordinary sign to attract the attention of the pupils; then he will indicate with the point of the signal the rule which the pupil has violated and immediately make a sign to the pupil to draw near. The pupil will go to the teacher, make the sign of the cross, and hold out his hand. Care will be taken that the pupil holds his hand well extended and quite steady and that he does not withdraw it. If he does not hold his hand well extended and quite steady, the teacher will, by extending his own hand, make him a sign to hold it well. If after that he does not comply, he must be forced to do so and given two strokes of the ferule instead of one.

If, when the teacher wishes to make a pupil hold out his hand, he meets with resistance, he will make a sign to the pupil to go to the place where punishment is administered and will there administer it to him, conducting himself as he has been told to do when he punishes with the rod, etc.

He will take care when he gives the ferule that the pupil does not put his thumb in the middle of his hand and that he does not hold his hand half open. Afterward, he will oblige him to cross his arms and kneel, or he will send him in a decorous manner to his seat, without permitting him to make any contortions with his arm or his body or to do anything else unseemly—such as grumbling or crying aloud. If it happens that he does any of these things, he will make him come back to him and will again give him the ferule, unless he at once ceases doing whatever improper thing he has been doing.

When the teacher wishes to administer punishment to a pupil with the rod, he will make the ordinary sign to attract the attention of the pupils; then he will indicate with the point of the signal the rule that the pupil has violated and immediately point to the place where it is the custom to receive this punishment.

The pupil will at once go there and prepare to receive it, holding himself in such a manner that he may not appear indecently to anyone. This practice of having the pupil prepare to receive the punishment, without the teacher having need to lay his hand upon him, will be very rigorously observed; and if any pupil fails to do this, he will be severely punished.

While the pupil is making ready to receive the punishment, the teacher will prepare himself inwardly to administer it in a spirit of charity and with his thoughts fixed on God. Then he will gravely and sedately leave his place.

When he reaches the place where the pupil is, he may say to him a few words to dispose him to receive the punishment with humility, submission, and the intention of correcting himself. After this, he will give the three usual blows.

He will be careful not to lay his hand on the pupil for any reason whatsoever while he is punishing him. If the pupil is not then ready, he will return to his place without saying anything; and when he comes back he will give him more than the ordinary punishment; that is to say, he will give him five blows with the rod.

All the pupils will be instructed that they must be ready

to receive the punishment before the teacher comes and that if they are not then ready, they will receive five blows.

The teacher will go back to his place and remain there quietly. A little while later, he will return to the pupil, and if he is not yet submissive and has not rearranged himself, he will act in the same manner in respect to him as has been said above in respect to stubborn pupils. He will be careful, however, in such encounters, to unite moderation with firmness.

When he has been thus obliged to constrain a pupil to receive punishment, he will manage in some way at some later time to make him recognize and admit his fault. He will make him reflect and will bring him to a strong and sincere resolution never to let himself yield again to a similar obstinacy.

After the pupil has been punished, he will go and kneel decorously in the middle of the classroom in front of the teacher, to thank him for having punished him; and he will then turn toward the crucifix, to thank God and to promise Him at the same time not to fall again into the fault for which he has been punished. He will do this without speaking aloud. After this, the teacher will make him a sign to go to his place.

ARTICLE VII

The Place for Administering Punishments. When They Should and When They Should Not Be Administered

A teacher must never leave his place to give the ferule; and if he should happen to be elsewhere, he will return there for this purpose.

Ordinary punishments with the rod will be administered in one of the most remote and obscure places in the classroom, where any exposure of the pupil who is being punished cannot be perceived by the others. Great care must be taken in regard to this matter and also to inspire the pupils with a great horror of the least glance on these occasions. Extraordinary punishments, which are inflicted for certain particular faults that are very grave in comparison with others—such, for instance, as stealing, disobeying and resisting the teacher—should be publicly administered, that is to say, in the presence of the pupils and in the middle of the classroom, in order to give an example and to make a greater impression. It would even be useful to punish a pupil sometimes in all the classrooms for very considerable and extraordinary faults.

Punishments must not be administered during Catechism or during the prayers. What the teacher may do during these times is to take particular note of those who have committed some fault, saying nothing to them but naming them in a low tone to a reliable pupil, with instructions to remind him at another time which he will indicate. He may, however, sometimes, but rarely, give the ferule during Catechism, if he believes that it cannot be avoided. Neither must punishments be inflicted on Sundays and holy days.

It is well to punish only in the afternoon rather than in the morning and never at the end of school.

It is also very important to do nothing in church or on the street that savors of punishment—such, for example, as to strike with the hand or to pull the ear or the arm. These are things which indicate impatience and are very contrary to the gravity and wisdom which a teacher should always show, particularly in these places.

PENANCES: THEIR USE, THEIR QUALITIES, AND THE MANNER OF IMPOSING THEM

Penances will be much more ordinarily used in the schools than punishments. They repel the pupil less, cause less distress to parents, and are much more useful.

The teachers will make use of them to humble their pupils and to bring them to a state of heart to correct themselves of their faults.

They should be remedial and proportioned to the faults which the pupils have committed, in order that they may help to give satisfaction for them in the sight of God, and even that they may be a preservative remedy to prevent repetition of the faults.

They will take great care that the penances that they impose be in no way ridiculous nor consist only of words, and to require them to be performed only in the classroom in which the pupil who has committed the fault is.

No penance will be imposed that might be prejudicial to the silence and order of the school. Nothing that causes loss of time and is of no utility should ever be given as a penance.

The teachers will impose no other penances than those which are in use in the schools and which are indicated in the following section. They will not impose extraordinary penances unless they have previously submitted them to the Brother Director, and he has given his consent.

When the teacher imposes a penance on some pupil, he will do so seated at his own place and in a very grave manner, such as may inspire respect in the one who receives the penance and make him perform it with humility and to the edification of the others.

When he wishes to impose a penance on a pupil, he will make him the ordinary sign to go kneel in the middle of the classroom; and then after clasping his own hands as a sign to the pupil to clasp his, he will gravely pronounce the penance, naming the fault for which he is imposing it. He will not say a single word more than the penance requires, using the following or similar terms, in a loud, grave, and intelligible tone: "For having come to school late today, you will be among the first to come during the period of a week; and if you fail to do so, you will be punished." To do this effectively, it should be done when the pupil is thinking of it the least.

After the teacher has imposed the penance, the pupil will make a bow to thank him and then will remain some little time longer kneeling, turned toward the crucifix, to evidence to God that he accepts the penance willingly and to ask of Him the grace to perform it faithfully and for the love of Him. Then he will return to his seat if he has permission to do so.

When penances are assigned to be performed at another time than that at which they are imposed, the teacher will charge some of the pupils to watch over the one to whom he has given the penance, to observe whether he performs it or not and to inform him without fail.

CORRECTIONS

Section I

List of Penances Which Are in Use and Can Be Imposed on the Pupils for Certain Faults

When a pupil comes late through his own fault a second time, instead of punishing him, he may be required as a penance to be at school during a period of a week or two as soon as the door is opened; and the Inspector of the Class will be instructed to notice whether he is there or not.

When a pupil is engrossed in eating to such an extent that he does not listen with attention as he should to the prayers, to the responses of Holy Mass, or to the Catechism, he will be made to kneel for a certain time.

When a pupil makes several mistakes in reading, because he has not studied, he may be ordered to learn by heart something from the Diocesan Catechism or even a part of the lesson which he has not studied—which would be very appropriate—or he may be ordered to read one or two pages, according to his ability, after all the others have read, at the same time threatening him with punishment if he does not know his lesson better. He will be required to read more or less, according to the section of the grade in which he is.

When a pupil does not follow during a lesson, he may be required as a penance to hold his book before his eyes for the period of half an hour without looking elsewhere.

As for those who have not written all that they should write or who have not applied themselves to doing it well, they may be required, as a penance, to write one or two pages at home, consisting of some particular letters, words, or phrases that have been indicated to them, which they must take pains to write well and bring the next time.

In regard to those who have been lacking in decorum during the prayers or who have not prayed to God, they may be ordered to stand in the middle of the classroom during the prayers for one or more days, their hands clasped, their eyes lowered, and with great decorum, on the condition that if they raise their eyes or commit any other breach of decorum, they will be punished.

The same will be done in respect to those who have been lacking in decorum in church; that is to say, they may be ordered to keep their hands clasped throughout all the time of Holy Mass the next day, without turning their heads or raising their eyes, and other similar things.

When a pupil who is kneeling seats himself on his heels, he will be required to remain about half an hour kneeling in school, or he will be made to remain standing for some time, with his hands clasped, his eyes lowered or resting on the crucifix.

Likewise, those who lean on the table or who maintain lax or unseemly postures will also be made to stand.

When a pupil has not retained the Catechism lesson of the preceding day, he will be obliged to learn it and repeat it at the end of school, without making a mistake or omitting anything; or he will be obliged to listen to the lesson of the day, standing, with his hands clasped; or else he may be made to learn on one day one or two lessons in the Catechism, according to his capacity.

When a pupil does not know perfectly the Catechism lesson which he ought to learn during the week, he will be obliged to learn it and repeat it on Monday or Tuesday and to know it perfectly without making a single mistake in it, under penalty of a double punishment and of continuing to do the same penance the following week.

To punish class officers for not having properly acquitted themselves of their duties, they may be deposed for some days and made to suffer some humiliation.

The most appropriate penance and the one that is of the greatest utility is to give the pupils something to learn by heart.

CHAPTER VI

Absences

ARTICLE I

Regular Absences and Absences with Permission

There are some pupils who ask permission to be absent regularly on every day in the week for a certain length of time each day. This may be accorded them in moderation and for the following reasons, after they have been carefully investigated:

Certain pupils may be sometimes permitted to absent themselves from school during the week, for example, on market days to go to work or on account of their employment, provided it be not in the afternoon and that it be to work and for nothing else. Some may be allowed, for the same reason, to come to school in the afternoon every day. However, no pupil will be permitted to come to school only in the morning. It will also not be permitted any pupil to come only at nine o'clock in the morning or at three o'clock in the afternoon, because, besides the fact that this disturbs the order of a school, many would wish to do the same. Neither must others be allowed to come to school in the afternoon and to go away before the Catechism. All the pupils will be obliged to be present at the Catechism as well as at the prayers every day. Nevertheless, for weighty reasons, those pupils who work may sometimes be permitted, and even regularly those of the writing class, to come in as soon as school begins in the morning, in order to read or to write, and to go away before the end of school, provided they come also in the afternoon and are present at the Catechism and the prayers.

ARTICLE II

IRREGULAR ABSENCES AND THOSE THAT MAY OR MAY NOT BE PERMITTED

It sometimes happens that the pupils ask permission to be absent on Sundays and holy days, some to go on trips or to go to visit their relatives; others to go to some village celebration or to some confraternity. None will be permitted to absent themselves from the Catechism on Sundays and holy days for any of these reasons, except upon rare occasions and when their parents ask it for them.

On school days, pupils will be permitted to go on pilgrimages at a distance from the town and at which there is ordinarily a great concourse of people, when they go with their parents and when it is evident that it is only devotion and piety which actuate them; but they will not be allowed to absent themselves from school to be present at processions, except that of the Blessed Sacrament during the octave of the feast, if it happens to be held in some parish on a day on which school is kept.

The pupils will be permitted to absent themselves from school on the feast of the Patron Saint of the parish in which they live, provided it be a solemn feast and celebrated by the parishioners.

Pupils whose fathers follow a trade may be permitted to absent themselves from school on the feast of the Patron Saint of their fathers' trade; however, they will be required to come to school in the afternoon.

Children will be permitted to absent themselves from school in order to buy stockings, shoes, etc., and even to mend their clothes, when it appears absolutely necessary, and the parents cannot choose another time.

No pupil will be permitted to absent himself on Monday and Tuesday before Lent. This practice, which should be considered of very great importance, will be very rigorously observed.

ARTICLE III

The Causes of Absences and the Means of Preventing Them

When pupils are frequently absent from school, it is through their own fault, through that of their parents, or through the fault of the teachers.

The first cause of the absences of pupils proceeds from the pupils themselves, on account of frivolousness, of wildness, or because they have a distaste for school and little affection for their teacher or dislike him.

Those who stay away through frivolousness are those who follow the first idea that comes into their minds, who go to play with the first child they meet, and who ordinarily act without paying attention to what they do.

It is very difficult for pupils of this sort not to absent themselves from time to time. All that can be done is to manage in such a way that their absences be rare and of short duration.

Such pupils should receive little punishment for their absences, because, on the next day or on the first occasion afterward, they will again absent themselves, reflecting neither upon what has been said to them nor upon the punishment that they have received. They will be induced to come to school more by gentleness and by winning them than by punishment and harshness.

The teachers will take care to stimulate from time to time children with this type of mind, to encourage them by some reward or by some outside employment, if they are capable of undertaking it. Above all, they will never threaten them with punishment.

The second reason why pupils absent themselves is wildness, either because they cannot be subjected to remaining thus a whole day in the same place, attentive, with their minds busy, or because they love to run about and to play. Such children are ordinarily inclined to evil; and viciousness follows wildness. For this reason, it is necessary to seek with very great care a remedy for their absences; and everything should be done to anticipate and to prevent them. It will be very useful to assign to them some office; this will give them a liking for school and sometimes even will cause them to become an example to the others. Much must be done to win them and to attract them, otherwise being firm with them and punishing them when they do wrong or absent themselves, but showing them much affection for the little good they do and rewarding them for little.

The third reason why pupils absent themselves is because they acquire a distaste for school. This may be due to the fact that they have a new teacher who is not yet sufficiently trained and does not know how to conduct himself in a school, but at once resorts to punishments, or because he is too lax and has no order or silence in his classroom.

The remedy for absences of this sort is not to leave a teacher alone in a classroom, and not to give him entire charge of one until he has been thoroughly trained by some Brother of great experience in the schools.

This practice is of very great importance, both for the welfare of the teachers and of the pupils and to prevent frequent absences as well as various other disorders.

In regard to teachers who are lax and who have no order in their classrooms, the remedy will be that the Brother Director or the Head Teacher watch over them and require them to account for all that takes place in their classes—above all, when they have neglected to look after the absent or have been remiss in one of their duties, however small and of however little consequence it may appear.

The fourth reason why pupils absent themselves is that they have little affection for their teacher, who is not prepossessing and who does not know how to win them, and, as on almost every occasion he resorts only to severity and punishments, the children are unwilling to come to school.

The remedies for this sort of absence will be for the teachers to endeavor to render themselves very prepossessing and to acquire a polite, affable, and frank appearance, without, however, assuming an undignified or familiar manner. Let them do everything for all their pupils to win them all to Our Lord Jesus Christ; for they should all be convinced that authority is acquired and maintained in a school more by firmness, gravity, and silence than by blows and harshness and that the principal cause of the frequent absences is the frequency of the punishments.

The fifth principal reason for the absence of pupils is due to their parents, either because they neglect to send them to school, not taking much trouble to make them come or be assiduous—which is quite ordinary among the poor—or because they themselves are indifferent to school, persuading themselves that their children learn very little or nothing there.

The means of remedying the negligence of parents, above all of the poor children, is to speak to them and make them understand the obligation under which they are of having their children taught, the wrong that they do them in not making them learn to read and write, and how much that can harm them, as for lack of this knowledge they will never be capable of any employment. Then, they must be made to understand the harm that may be done their children by lack of instruction in those things which concern their salvation—with which the poor are often little concerned. Secondly, since this kind of poor are ordinarily those who receive alms, a list should be given to the parish priests of all those who do not come to school, their ages, their dwellings, in order that no alms be given their parents and that they may be urged and obliged to send their children to school. Thirdly, an effort must be made to attract the children of persons of this sort and to win them by every possible means, which can often be done with success; for ordinarily the children of the poor do as they wish, their parents having no care of them and even idolizing them, so that what their children want they also want. Thus, it is enough that their children should want to come to school for them to be content to send them there.

When parents withdraw their children from school to make them work while they are too young and not yet sufficiently instructed, they should be made to understand that they harm them a great deal and that in order to have them earn a little they will make them lose a very much more considerable advantage. It should be represented to them of what importance it is to an artisan to know how to read and write well, since, however little intelligent he may be, if he knows how to read and write he is capable of anything.

Parents must be urged to send their children to school, if not the whole day, at least the entire afternoon. It will be necessary to watch very especially over children of this sort and take care of them. If it happens that the parents complain because their children learn only little or nothing and wish to withdraw them for this reason, to obviate this inconvenience the Brothers Directors or the Inspectors of Schools must watch with great care over all the teachers under their direction, particularly those of lesser ability. They must see that they instruct as diligently as possible all the pupils who are intrusted to them; that they neglect none and that they apply themselves equally to them all, even more to the more ignorant and more negligent; that they keep order in the schools and that the pupils do not absent themselves frequently, the liberty in respect to being absent which they are allowed being often the cause of their learning nothing.

The sixth principal reason why pupils absent themselves frequently is because the teachers are too complacent in bearing with those who are absent from school without permission, or because they too readily give permission to be absent.

To provide a remedy for this inconvenience, every teacher must be very exact in watching over those who go to visit the absent. He must make sure that they go to the homes of all of them, that they do not let themselves be deceived by false reasons, and that they afterward report to the teacher the reasons that have been given them. Secondly, let him who receives the pupils who have been absent and excuses their absences require their parents to bring them back, and let him receive no pupil who has been absent without knowing and investigating well the reason that he gives for his absence.

The ordinary reasons are that their parents needed them, that they have been ill, or that they have absented themselves through wildness.

In respect to the first reason, in order for it to be good and valid, the need must be great, and it must be very rare. As for the second reason, the Inspector or the teacher will not admit it if the pupil has been seen outside his house or playing with other children. Every teacher will take care that those who visit the homes of the absent see all the ill pupils and report on the state in which they find them.

So far as the truants are concerned, the Inspector or the teacher will observe what has been said above in the article on pupils who must or must not be punished; and they will not punish them themselves, but will oblige their parents to punish them at home before permitting them to return to school.

As for those who have been absent without permission under the pretext that their parents needed them, they must not be easily excused; and as it is ordinarily the same ones who are guilty of this fault, if they repeat it three or four times without troubling themselves about it, they must be sent away and not received again until they are disposed, as well as their parents, to ask permission every time they absent themselves.

When the pupils ask permission to absent themselves, the teachers must always appear unaccommodating in respect to such permissions. Let them investigate well the reasons, and in case they find them good and necessary, they will always send the pupil to the Head Teacher to obtain the permission, which he will, however, grant only with great difficulty; and he will never listen to a pupil who asks for a permission that the teacher has refused.

Absences will be rare unless they are for trivial reasons; and it is of this that the teachers must be very careful. It is better to send pupils away than to permit them to absent themselves frequently, as they set a very bad example. Three or four will be found in a school who ask permission to absent themselves; and if it is accorded them, they will cause the others to absent themselves without reason. It is better to send away pupils of this sort and to have fifty who are very assiduous than a hundred who are absent at every moment.

However, before sending pupils away for such reasons— or even for other reasons—the teacher will speak with their parents several times, to represent to them how important it is that their children should come to school assiduously and that it is otherwise almost impossible for them to learn anything, since they forget in one day what they have learned in several. Pupils will not be sent away from school unless it appears that both they and their parents do not trouble about it and do not profit at all by all that it has been possible to say to them on the subject.

Finally, before sending away pupils on account of absences or for anything else, it is well to make use of the following means to remedy the situation: 1. Deprive a pupil who has been absent—even with permission—of all the rewards that would have been given to him if he had been assiduous. 2. Do not promote him to another section or to another grade the next month, even though he should know how to read perfectly or should be capable of being promoted. 3. Make him stand for several days in school, or make use of some other penance that will humiliate him and will be unpleasant for his parents, so as to incite him to come punctually and to oblige his parents to force him to be assiduous.

ARTICLE IV

How and by Whom Absentees Should Be Received, and Their Absences Excused

The Brother Director will appoint one teacher in each school to receive pupils who have been absent and to excuse their absences.

Pupils who have been absent may be received and their absences excused not later than half past eight in the morning and, in the afternoon, not later than two o'clock. The teachers will not fail to notify the pupils that all who have been absent must be at school before they themselves arrive there, and that if their absences have not been excused before the bell begins to ring at half past eight in the morning and at two o'clock in the afternoon, no matter what reasons they allege, they will be punished or sent away.

If parents make complaints when they bring back their children, he who receives them will be careful always to excuse the teacher, if it is of him that complaints are made; and he will then give them whatever advice he judges necessary. He will take care to report later to the Brother Director the complaints that have been made to him and the reason for which they were made. He who excuses absentees will be careful to finish with the parents in few words.

If it is through the fault of the parents that the pupil has been absent, the pupil will be made to enter the school, and then the teacher who has received them will speak with the parents in private, in order to make them realize their fault and the wrong that they are doing their children in procuring permission for them or allowing them to absent themselves; and he will urge them to be more exact in making the children come to school assiduously, informing them that if they fail to do so again for similar reasons, the children will not be taken back, which, in reality, must be the case.

If the pupil is absent through his own fault, he must be reprimanded in the presence of the parent who brings him, to whom will be given later, in private, the necessary instructions for forestalling and preventing the absences of the child.

If the teacher who is to excuse the absence is not familiar with the conduct of the pupil and the reasons for his absence, or if he is in doubt concerning them, he will leave the parent and the pupil at the door and go to inquire of the teacher of the pupil; he will then return to speak with them and will tell them what he considers proper.

When pupils who have absented themselves or who have been excused enter school, they will stand at the back of the classroom until the teacher who has excused their absences has spoken to the teacher of their class and the latter has instructed them to go to their seats or to the bench of the absentees.

When the teacher who is appointed to excuse the pupils has excused the absentees who have presented themselves each time, he will go or send someone to tell each teacher which pupils have been brought back, what their parents have said to him, in what manner and under what conditions he has received them.

CHAPTER VII

Holidays

It is important that holidays and vacations should always be regulated in the same manner in all the schools. This is one of the things that will be of great use in maintaining good order.

There are four things to be considered in this chapter: 1. Ordinary holidays. 2. Extraordinary holidays and the occasions on which they may or may not be given. 3. Vacation. 4. Manner of indicating and making known holidays, both to teachers and to pupils.

Ordinary Holidays

Ordinary holidays are those that are indicated below.

A whole holiday will be given every Thursday of each week in the year, if there are no holy days of obligation during the week.

When there is a holy day of obligation in a week, if it falls on Monday, Tuesday, or Saturday, a half holiday will be given Thursday afternoon; if it falls on Thursday or Friday, a half holiday will be given Tuesday afternoon; and if it falls on Wednesday, a half holiday will be given on Friday afternoon.

When there are two or more holy days of obligation in a week, there will be no holiday in that week.

On the day of the Feast of Saint Nicholas, who is the Patron Saint of school children, and on Ash Wednesday, a whole holiday will be given instead of on the Thursday of that week. However, on each of these days, the pupils will be made to come to school in the morning, and they will be taught their Catechism from eight to nine o'clock, when they will be taken to Holy Mass in the church to which it is the custom to take them.

On Ash Wednesday, after Holy Mass, they will receive the ashes. If there is an interval between the prayers in school and the time for Holy Mass, the pupils will be instructed by demonstration concerning what they should do and how they should approach the altar to receive the ashes. If there is no interval between the prayers and Holy Mass, these instructions will be given during the last quarter of an hour of the Catechism.

If the Feast of Saint Nicholas falls on a Sunday, the celebration of it will be transferred for the pupils to the following Thursday, which will be observed as indicated above.

On the day of the Feast of Saint Joseph, who is the Patron Saint of the Community,* a whole holiday will be given instead of on Thursday; and when this feast falls on Sunday or in Holy Week, it will be celebrated on the day to which it is transferred by the Church.

Holiday will be given from Thursday in Holy Week, inclusive, to the following Wednesday, exclusive, on which day school will begin again. However, the pupils will be taken to the Parochial Mass on the two last-named feasts,† and they will be taught their Catechism on the days of the feasts of the Transfiguration, of the Presentation and of the Visitation of the Blessed Virgin, and of the Exaltation of the Holy Cross.

On whatever day of the week these feasts come, holiday will be given instead of on Thursday; and no other holiday will be given during the week, unless one of the feasts comes on Sunday.

ARTICLE II

EXTRAORDINARY HOLIDAYS

No extraordinary holidays will be given without an evident and indispensable necessity; and when the Brother

* That is, of the Brothers of the Christian Schools.
† The Feast of Saint Joseph and Holy Thursday.

Director of a House thinks that he is obliged to give one, he will consult the Brother Superior of the Institute before doing so, in case he can foresee it; or, if he cannot foresee it, he will inform him afterward, making known the reasons that have obliged him to give this holiday.

When it is necessary to give an extraordinary holiday, it will always be given instead of the regular weekly holiday. If there is a holy day in the week, the extraordinary holiday will be given only in the afternoon, in case the necessity be only for the afternoon; but if the necessity be for the morning, the holiday will be given for the whole day.

The occasions on which extraordinary holidays will be given are the following:

First, fair days, when they last only one day.

Second, the day of the burial of a Brother who has died in the Brothers' House in the town. If it is not possible to celebrate the Funeral Office either the next day or in the same week, a whole holiday will be given on the day of the burial instead of on Thursday. If it is possible to celebrate the office the next day, a whole holiday will also be given then. If the Funeral Office is celebrated in the same House on a day much later than that of the burial or in another week, on the day of the Office a whole holiday will be given.

Third, holiday will be given on the days on which some extraordinary ceremony is being celebrated in the town; provided it be not bad or that it will do the pupils no harm to be there, and it is not considered possible to prevent them from going.

Fourth, holiday will be given on the day of the feast of the Patron Saint of each of the parishes in which the schools are situated, as also on certain days which, while they are neither days upon which it is necessary to refrain from servile work nor holy days of obligation, are nevertheless kept in the town or in the parish in which is situated the House of the Institute.

Fifth, holiday will also be given on the day of the octave of the Most Blessed Sacrament,* even though there be a holy day in that week.

The occasions on which neither ordinary nor extraordinary holidays will be given are the following:

First, the Monday and Tuesday immediately preceding the first day of Lent; and the pupils will even be required to be more exact in their attendance at school on these days than on any other day in the year.

Second, Rogation Days and the Feast of Saint Mark, under pretext of assisting at the processions.

Third, the Feast of the Translation of Saint Nicholas, without consideration for the fact that it is one of the feasts of the Patron Saint of school children.

Fourth, the days of the feasts of the Patron Saints of the different trades or any one of them.

The time spent in school will not be diminished, unless for some evident and unavoidable necessity.

ARTICLE III

Vacation

This article comprises four things: 1. Things concerning the vacation in itself. 2. The counsel that the teachers should give their pupils, so that they may pass the vacation time well. 3. What is to be done in school on the last day before

* The Feast of Corpus Christi.

vacation. 4. What is to be done on the day of the return to school.

Every year, school will cease everywhere during one month; and this is what is called vacation.

Vacation will be given everywhere during the month of September; and all will also return to school everywhere on the first of October.

On the last day of school, nothing will be done from one o'clock until half past three except the Catechism; and this will be on the manner in which the pupils should pass the time of their vacation. Among the counsels which the teachers will give the pupils so that they may pass this time well, the principal are: 1. Not to fail to say each day the morning and evening prayers that are recited in the schools. 2. To assist at Holy Mass daily with devotion and to say throughout Holy Mass the prayers which are in the Manual of Exercises of Piety. 3. To assist at the High Mass and Vespers in their parish churches on Sundays and holy days of obligation. 4. To go to Confession and, for those who have already made their First Communion, to go to Holy Communion at least once during this time. 5. To go each day to some church to visit and adore the Blessed Sacrament for at least a quarter or half of an hour. 6. To say the Rosary every day, in order to acquire and preserve a devotion to the Blessed Virgin. 7. Not to frequent bad company. 8. Not to plunder gardens and vineyards, which would be thieving and a great sin. 9. Not to go bathing.* 10. Not to play cards or dice for money.

At three o'clock, the prayers will be said; then the teachers

---

* This, of course, refers to bathing in public and probably nude.

will return their papers to the writers, in order that they may practice writing during the vacation, and they will even urge them to do so. No rewards will be given at this time; this will be postponed until after the vacation, at the opening of school—unless the Brother Director sees fit to do otherwise.

At the end of the Catechism, the teachers will notify all the pupils to be in school on the appointed day as early as half past seven o'clock in the morning, in order to assist at the Mass of the Holy Ghost, which will be celebrated for their intention.* On that day, while they are assembling in school, they will be taught the Catechism from eight until nine o'clock, after the prayers which are said at the opening of school.

At nine o'clock they will be taken to Holy Mass, which will be celebrated for their intention, to invoke the assistance of the Holy Ghost.

The pastors of the parishes in which the schools are situated will be requested to say this special Mass or to have it said; otherwise, it will be said at the expense of the House.

ARTICLE IV

MANNER OF INFORMING TEACHERS AND PUPILS OF HOLIDAYS

Every Sunday, at the end of the thanksgiving after Holy Communion, the Brother Director of each House will announce to the Brothers the holy days of obligation that will occur during the coming week, the day on which there will

---

* Wherever Catholic civilization dominates, it is customary to celebrate this Mass in honor of the Holy Ghost, to invoke the divine inspiration and aid, at the opening of schools, parliaments, courts of justice, deliberative assemblies, etc.

be holiday, and whether it will be a whole holiday or in the afternoon only.

If it happens that it is necessary to give some extraordinary holiday which he has not foreseen on Sunday, he will give notice of it the evening before or in the morning after the litany of the Holy Child Jesus or else in the afternoon immediately after the litany of Saint Joseph. If there is anything particular to be done in school during the week, he will follow the same procedure.

Each teacher will announce in his own classroom, at the end of school, immediately after evening prayers, the holidays and any other special events—above all, the fasts of the Church—that occur during the week. He will take care to state these things in few words, to forget nothing, and to express them in such a manner that they can be understood by all the pupils.

CHAPTER VIII

School Officers

There will be several officers in the school, charged with various different functions which the teachers cannot do or ought not to do themselves.

These officers will be appointed by the teachers in each class on one of the first three school days after the vacation.

Each teacher will submit the names of those whom he has chosen to the Brother Director or to the Head Teacher, and he will not have them enter upon the exercise of their duties until they have been approved. If it becomes necessary later to change them or to change one of them, the nomination of another or others will be made in the same manner. We shall speak below of these officers in order and of their obligation.

The Reciters of Prayers

There will be in each school two officers to whom will be assigned the duty of reciting the prayers, one of them in the morning and the other in the afternoon, who will be substituted in turn one for the other.

The one who says the prayers in the morning one week will say them in the afternoon the following week, and the other one will change in the same way. They will recite all the prayers that are said in school sedately, attentively, and decorously, in such a manner that they can be easily heard by all the pupils.

No pupil will be appointed to this office unless he knows perfectly all the prayers, unless he recites them distinctly, and unless he is reserved and well behaved, so as not to cause the pupils distractions.

These two Reciters will be appointed each month and will both be from the class of writers. They may be continued in office in case there are no others who can acquit themselves so well of this duty, but for no other reason; for this appointment contributes much to making the pupils recite the prayers well in private and to making them like to say them at home with deliberation and attention.

The Aspergill Bearer

There will be one pupil who will take an aspergill to Holy Mass on every school day and, on Sundays and holy days of obligation, to both Mass and Vespers, so that the pupils may take holy water on entering and leaving the church. This officer and the Keeper of Rosaries will go first and will lead the others on the way to church. On entering the church, the Aspergill Bearer will place himself near the holy-water font and will remain there until all the pupils of all the classes have passed and have taken holy water. He will do the same when the pupils leave the church. He will place himself in such a manner that the pupils can easily take holy water from the aspergill, which he will dip from time to time in the font, whenever he observes that there is no more holy water on it.

He will hold the aspergill straight out before him and will beware of using it to sprinkle or of playing with it, under pain of punishment.

As long as the pupils are passing, he will remain standing in a modest posture, his eyes lowered, without looking at any one of them as they are passing and without turning his head. When the pupils have left the church, if they do not return to the school, he will go there with the Keeper of Rosaries to replace the aspergill where it is usually kept. This pupil should be very pious and very well behaved; and he will not be replaced by another unless it is necessary.

The Keeper of Rosaries and His Assistants

There will be one pupil chosen to carry the rosaries to the church every time the pupils are taken there. The rosaries will be counted out to him by the teacher, and he will take care to count them every day immediately after Holy Mass or in the afternoon and if any of them are missing to notify the teacher, who will count them himself on the last school day of each week. There will be as many bunches of rosaries as there are ranks in the church of two pupils in a row, and if there is more than one rank of two in a row, there will be one or more assistants to distribute the rosaries, one to each rank of two pupils in a row.

When the pupils are all kneeling in their places, this officer will take one or more bunches of rosaries, which he will give to his assistant or assistants, and each one of them will go down a rank between two pupils from top to bottom, to distribute the rosaries to those who do not know how to read, that is to say, to those who are learning the charts of the alphabet and of the syllables.

As soon as Holy Mass is finished, they will go in the same way, each one down the rank that has been assigned to him, to take back the rosaries from those to whom they have given them at the beginning of Holy Mass, and the Keeper of Rosaries will then take the bunches from his assistants and add them to his own.

If the pupils do not return to the school after Holy Mass, the Keeper of Rosaries will go with the Aspergill Bearer to take the rosaries back to the school and put them in their usual place.

It will also be the duty of this officer to give, every day at the beginning of school, both morning and afternoon, the rosaries to those who are to be the first to say the Rosary in school; and he will take care to remember those who were the last to say it during the preceding session of school.

He will instruct the pupils to say it in turn, in the order of the benches, and he will see that those who say the Rosary in school say it with deliberation, piety, and decorum, that they do not talk and play; and if he notices that they are guilty of any of these things, he will at once inform the teacher.

If there are more than three classes in a school, there will be two or three pupils appointed to this office. This officer should be very sensible, very well behaved, and even very trustworthy, so that he may be careful not to mislay the rosaries.

He and his assistants will ordinarily be chosen from the class in which the Rosary is said; but if there are not any in it who are capable, he will be chosen from another.

The Bell Ringer

There will be in each school a pupil whose function will be to ring the bell for the beginning of school and of the exercises. He will ring, at the beginning of school and at every hour, five separate, clear, and distinct strokes; every half hour, he will tinkle five or six strokes; at the end of school, he will ring the bell and then tinkle five or six strokes also, to make known that it is the end of school and that the prayers are to begin. He will be careful to ring exactly on time: about the time for a *Miserere* before the beginning of the prayers in the morning and before the Catechism in the afternoon, when he will tinkle two or three strokes to notify the pupils to put their books away, the Collectors of Papers to gather up all papers, and all to prepare themselves and be ready to begin the prayers, without a moment's delay, as soon as the bell has ceased ringing. This officer should be very assiduous in attending school, careful, vigilant, exact, and very punctual in ringing on time.

CONDUCT OF THE SCHOOLS

Inspectors and Supervisors

There will be Inspectors in all the classes during the absences of the teachers but at no other times, except in the classes of the writers, in which there will be an Inspector during breakfast and lunch, who will supervise the one or the ones who are repeating the prayers, the Catechism, and the responses of Holy Mass.

All the care and attention of the Inspector will be directed to observing everything that takes place in the classroom, without saying a single word, no matter what happens, and without leaving his place; nor will he permit any pupil to speak to him or to approach him during the entire time that he is fulfilling his duties.

He will not threaten any pupil, either by signs or otherwise, no matter what fault he commits. He will never make use of the ferule or of anything whatsoever to strike the pupils.

He will remain all the time seated at the place that has been assigned to him, and he will report faithfully to the teacher everything just as it has happened, without adding or concealing anything. He will notice those who keep silent and those who make the least noise, and above all he will take care to give a good example to the others; for he must be persuaded that he has been put there not only to watch all that takes place in the school but even more to be the model which the others are to imitate.

The teacher will examine carefully the things that the Inspector reports to him (in a low tone and privately) before determining whether or not he ought to punish those who have been denounced to him for having committed faults.

In order to find out more easily whether the Inspector has told the truth, he will ask privately the most trustworthy pupils who have witnessed the faults whether the matter took place in the manner and under the circumstances that the Inspector has declared; and he will punish the pupils who have committed the faults only in case he finds that what the others say agrees with what the Inspector has reported.

The teacher will listen to complaints that are made against the Inspector, especially if those who make them are disinterested, and if they are among the more sensible and more trustworthy pupils. Should the Inspector be found guilty, he will be much more severely punished than another would be for the same fault, and will at once be deprived of his office.

The Inspector must be very punctual and among the first to come to school. He must be vigilant, so as to observe all that takes place in the school. He must be neither frivolous nor a liar, and he must not be capable of partiality for anyone, so that he would accuse his brothers, his friends, and his companions—that is, those with whom he associates—as well as the others. Above all, he must not receive any gift from anyone; and if he is detected in this fault, he will be very severely punished and deprived of his office.

Supervisors

There will be in each class two pupils appointed to watch the conduct of the Inspector while he is exercising his functions, in order to see whether he allows himself to be corrupted by gifts; whether he demands anything from the others for not declaring their faults; whether he is always among the first to come to school; whether he speaks; whether he leaves his place; whether he sees to it that no one else leaves his; in short, whether he fulfills his duties with very great exactitude. It will be very much to the purpose if these Supervisors are not known to the Inspector; and for this reason, they will not be appointed like the other officers and will not even be called officers. The Supervisors will be among the most sensible, the most pious, and the most punctual pupils, who will be privately instructed to pay attention to the conduct of the Inspector; and they will render an account of it as soon as possible whenever anything extraordinary happens.

There will also be certain Inspectors or Supervisors for the streets—especially for those in which many pupils live—who will observe in what manner the pupils of this district behave when returning from school.

There will be some of them in each district or important street, who will observe everything that takes place and will at once notify the teacher of it in private.

Distributors and Collectors of Papers

There will be in the class of the writers one or two pupils whose care it will be to distribute the papers to the writers at the beginning of the writing period, to take them again at the end of it, and then to put them back in the proper place.

If all the pupils in the class are learning to write, there will be two charged with this function; if only a part of them, and they are not too numerous, there will be only one.

The Distributors and Collectors of Papers will be careful to place the papers all in order one upon another, in the same order as are seated the pupils to whom they belong, so that they may return them all with accuracy.

They will go from table to table, both to give them out and to take them back—if any pupil is absent, they will leave his paper at his place—and they will be sure to distribute and collect them promptly and silently.

If the teacher finds it desirable, a short time before collecting the papers, these officers will go to each writer to see what he has written—whether he has written as much as he should; whether the paper is rumpled, etc. If they find that anyone has been remiss in anything, they will at once inform the teacher of it.

They will make sure that all the pupils dry what they have written and fold their papers before returning them.

Sweepers

There will be one pupil in each classroom whose duty will be to sweep it and keep it clean and neat. He will sweep it once daily without fail at the end of the morning school session; and if the pupils go to Holy Mass, he will return to the school for this purpose.

Before beginning to sweep, he will put the benches near the wall, some on one side and some on the other. In case there is any need of it, the two Sweepers from the two adjoining classrooms will help one another to remove and replace them but in nothing else.

After having removed the benches, he will sprinkle the floor of the classroom if it is necessary, and will then sweep it and carry all the rubbish in a basket to the street, to the place which is destined for this purpose. He will then replace the broom, the basket, and the other things that he has used in the place where they are ordinarily kept.

The teachers will see that the Sweepers keep always very clean the classrooms of which they have charge.

The Sweepers should not be slow, but must be very active, so that they will not take too much time in acquitting themselves of their duties.

They should be distinguished by a great care for neatness and cleanliness; but they must also be sensible and not given to quarreling or trifling.

The Doorkeeper

In each school, there will be only one entrance door; and if there be more than one door, the others—those which the Brother Director will select—will be closed and always kept locked.

There will be one pupil from one of the classrooms—ordinarily the one at the entrance—who will be appointed to open and shut this entrance door each time that anyone enters the school and who, for this reason, will be called the Doorkeeper.

He will be placed near the door, so that he may be able to open it promptly. He will not leave it open and will always bolt it.

He will allow no one to enter except the Brothers, the pupils, and the priest of the parish in which the school is situated.

When someone knocks at the door of the school, he will at once open it carefully, with the least possible delay, to answer the person who is knocking; and, after having again bolted the door, he will notify the teacher who is in the habit of speaking with visitors.

While the teacher is speaking with someone, the Doorkeeper will leave the door sufficiently open for it to be possible to see from within the classroom both the teacher and the person with whom he is speaking.

The Doorkeeper will guard the door from the time when it is opened until the pupils begin to leave the school. For this reason, he must always be the first to come. He will always keep silent and will never speak to any pupil who is entering or going out.

This officer will be exact in reading in his turn like the others, and he will apply himself to his lesson and follow all the time that he is not busy at the door. The Doorkeeper must be frequently changed if possible; and care should be taken that he does not lose his time, by making him read at the end of school or by having another take his place during his lessons.

This officer will also take charge of the stick which is given to the pupils when they go outside. He will give it to the one who is going out and will take care that no pupil goes out without having it, so that, in so far as possible, no two may go out together for this reason. He will put it away every day at the end of school, both in the morning and in the afternoon, and he will let no pupil go out unless he has the stick.

This pupil will be chosen from among the most diligent and the most regular in attendance at school. He should be sensible, reserved, well behaved, silent, and capable of edifying the people who come to knock at the door.

CONDUCT OF THE SCHOOLS

The Keeper of the Key

The Keeper of the Key will be at the door of the school punctually every day before half past seven in the morning and before one o'clock in the afternoon. He will be forbidden to give the key to any other pupil without the order of the Brother who is in charge of this school. If the pupils do not return to the school after Holy Mass, he will return there with the Keeper of Rosaries, the Aspergill Bearer, and the Sweepers. He will see that the latter make no noise while they are sweeping, and he will not leave the school before they sweep.

This pupil will also be in charge of the preservation of everything that is in the school, and he must take care that nothing is carried away. He should be chosen from among those who are the most assiduous at school and who never miss.

CHAPTER IX

Construction and Uniformity of Schools and of the Furniture Which They Contain

The schools should be arranged in such a manner that both the teachers and the pupils can easily fulfill their duties. The seats should be on the same level, both at the top and at the bottom. The entrance door, in so far as possible, should be placed in such a manner that the pupils need not pass through another classroom in order to reach their own.

SCHOOLS AND FURNISHINGS

When school is held in a room which opens upon the street or a common courtyard, care must be taken that the windows be at least seven feet above the ground, so that people passing may not be able to see into the school.

It must also be so arranged that there be certain conveniences for the children: there would be great disadvantages in their going out into the streets.

The classrooms must have good daylight and good air; and for that reason, there must be, if possible, windows at both ends of each one of them for ventilation.

The classrooms should be at least eighteen or twenty feet square or, at most, twenty-five, because classrooms that are very long or narrow are inconvenient.

The small and medium-sized classrooms should be at least fifteen to eighteen feet square; and the communicating door should be so situated that the teacher's chair can be placed against the wall opposite this door.

The benches of the pupils should be of different heights, that is, eight, ten, twelve, fourteen, and fifteen inches high; and they should be from twelve to fifteen feet long, entirely mortised. The boards of each bench should be about an inch and a half thick and six inches wide. Each bench should have three sets of feet, consisting of two uprights with a crossbar at the bottom. In each one of the lower classrooms, there should be two benches eight inches high for the smallest pupils; three, ten inches high; and three, twelve inches high for the medium-sized and larger ones. The number of these benches can be diminished or increased according to the number of the pupils.

In each large classroom, there should be a number of tables, corresponding to the number of the pupils, for writing exercises: two of the highest for the largest pupils, and the others lower for the medium sized and smallest, all with benches of the same length. The highest tables should be two feet three inches high at the back and two feet one inch at the front, in order to give a slope to the table. The benches for these tables should be fourteen inches high. The tops of the tables should be fifteen inches wide and at least an inch and a half thick. They should be nine, twelve, or fifteen feet in length, in proportion to the size of the class-room. Each table should be supported by three trestles or table supports. The top of each trestle should be as long as the table is wide, about three inches thick and five inches wide. The three uprights, which should be mortised into the top, should each be two inches square and should open out toward the bottom, where the spread should be of about fifteen inches, to give solidity and balance to the trestle. Each support should be attached to the table with a large square-headed screw, set in the table even with the surface, passing through it and the trestle, and fastened underneath with a bolt.

On the table, there will be as many leaden inkwells as necessary, each one to be used by two pupils. If, however, some Brother should later on find another manner of constructing these writing tables, which would be easier and more solid, he will propose it to the Brother Superior before making use of it.

The charts of the alphabet and of the syllables will be arranged in the following manner, and they will be the same in all the Houses of the Christian Schools:

SCHOOLS AND FURNISHINGS

PART I						PART II			
a	b	c	d	e		A	B	C	D	E
f	g	h	i	y		F	G	H	I	Y
j	l	m	n	o		J	K	L	M	N
p	q	r	s	ſ		P	Q	R	T	U
t	u	v	x	z		q	d	h	b	p
&	œ	æ	ct	ſt		A	FF	SST	M	h

MODEL OF CHART OF SYLLABLES

me	ca	et	eux	ce	ga	nos
em	gi	je	cho	of	cu	qui
œu	en	ei	l'hu	vu	go	ont
n'y	ge	in	gue	ha	on	sça
im	eu	xi	cun	ou	hé	pei
eſt	cé	el	gne	gu	j'i	nez
om	ex	ni	hau	co	ze	moy

These charts will be at least two feet four inches long and one foot eight inches high, not including the border.

The letters and syllables will be placed one above another in the form of a column, as is indicated above on the models of the two charts.

The chart of the alphabet will be divided into two parts, the first consisting of the small letters, and the second of the capital letters, as is indicated above. Each part will contain six lines; and each line, five letters, diphthongs and letters joined together being counted as only one letter, for example, ſt, ſl, fl, and the same with others. The table of small letters and the table of capital letters will be separated one from another by a space of about three inches, in such a manner that there will be a distance of three inches between the last letter of each line of the first part and the first letter of each line of the second part; for instance, there should be a distance of three inches between the small *e,* which is the last letter of the first line of the first part, and the capital *A,* which is the first letter of the first line of the second part; and the same with the others.

The first stroke of each letter in both parts should be at least an inch and two-thirds distance from the first stroke of the following one, and the lines should be at least three inches distant one from another.

The second chart, which is of syllables of two and of three letters should contain seven lines, and each line seven syllables. The first three, the fifth, and the sixth syllables of each line should be syllables of two letters; the fourth and seventh, of three letters, as is indicated on the above model. There must be at least two and two-thirds inches after each syllable, that is to say, between the end of a syllable and the beginning of the next; and the lines should be about three inches distant from each other.

The chart of Arabic and Roman numerals will be three feet eight inches in height and seven feet long. It will be divided into two panels.

In the first panel will be pasted a large sheet of paper, on which will be printed the Arabic and Roman numerals; and in the other, the vowels, the consonants, the punctuation marks, and the abbreviations.

SCHOOLS AND FURNISHINGS

Model of Chart of Arabic Numerals

Centaine de Million.	Dixaine de Million.	Million.	Centaine de Mille.	Dixaine de Mille.	Mille.	Centaine.	Dixaine.	Nombre.
								1.
							3.	2.
						5.	2.	3.
					6.	6.	5.	4.
				9.	8.	7.	6.	5.
			6.	3.	9.	8.	7.	6.
		6.	5.	6.	3.	9.	8.	7.
	2.	6.	3.	6.	1.	3.	9.	8.
1.	2.	3.	4.	5.	6.	7.	8.	9.
10.	11.	12.	13.	14.	15.	16.	17.	18.
19.	20.	35.	43.	51.	62.	73.	80.	93.
100.	1012.		12011.		1673167271.			

Model of Chart of Roman Numerals

C. D. I. L. M. V. X.

I.	XIII.	XC, C.	I^c.	XXXV.
II.	XIV.	CC.	II^c.	XLV.
III.	**XV.**	CCC.	III^c.	LXIV.
IV.	XIX.	CCCC.	IV^c.	XCIX.
V.	XX.	D.	V^c.	IC.
VI.	XXX.	DC.	VI^c.	ICC.
VII.	XL.	DCC.	VII^c.	ICCC.
VIII.	L.	DCCC.	VIII^c.	DCCC.
IX.	LX.	DCCCC.	IX^c.	ICCCCC.
X.	LXX.	M.CIC.	X^m.	XII^m.
XI.	IIII XX.*	XX m L m.	LXXIX m.	MM.
XII.	IIII xxX.*	CLXIV m.		

* *Quatre-vingts, quatre-vingt-dix.* Some of these combinations of Roman numerals appear out of the ordinary; they were, however, in use (see any good work on paleography, e. g., Maurice Prou, *Manuel de paléographie latine et française,* Paris, 1924).

CONDUCT OF THE SCHOOLS

VOYELLES

a, e, i, y, o, u.

CONSONNES

bé	cé	dé	effe	gé	ache	ca	el	eme	ene
b	c	d	f	g	h	k	l	m	n
pé	cu	er	esse	té	vé	icce	zede		
p	q	r	s	t	v	x	z		

PONCTUATIONS

Point .   deux points :   point & virgule ;   virgule ,
Interrogant ?   admiratif !
Où est Dieu?   O mon Dieu!

APOSTROPHE '

Il n'y a qu'un seul Dieu.

PARENTHÈSES ( )

Donnez (dit J. C.) & on vous donnera.

LIAISON

Y a-t-il,   est-il,   Très-saint.

ACCENT AIGU ´

Aimé, loüé, prisé, pensé, amitié.

ACCENT GRAVE

Près, Auprès, où, à, là.

ACCENT CIRCONFLEXE ^

Vôtre, même, maître, être.

SCHOOLS AND FURNISHINGS

E, I, U, AVEC DEUX POINTS DESSUS

Vuë, ruë, aïez, haïr, feüil, deüil.*

ABRÉVIATIONS

Deû, âte, nunquâ, ej′, utiq;, Dons.

There will also be in each classroom in which connected sentences are written a large board five feet in length and three feet in height, consisting of two panels on each of which can be written two examples in arithmetic, except examples in division, for which an entire panel will be required. This board should be attached to the wall in the most convenient place: the bottom about five feet above the floor, and the top slanting forward. The two panels of this board must be painted black with oil paint, in such a manner that it will be possible to write the examples upon them with chalk. The board should be of this form:

ADDITION		SUBTRACTION
214.1	14.9	4606504.1
3101.	15.6	2105063.
523.	10.3	————
————	————	
————	————	————

The chairs for the teachers in each classroom will measure twenty inches from the seat to the footstool, and the footstool, which will be attached to the chair, will be twelve inches in height; from the seat to the top of the back will be eighteen inches; the chairs will have straw bottoms.

* It will be readily noted that the use of some accents is not in conformity with present-day usage.

There will be a chest or cupboard in which to put away the papers and other things used by the teachers and pupils.

There will also be in each classroom a picture on paper of our Lord on the Cross; one of the Blessed Virgin; one of Saint Joseph; one representing the Holy Guardian Angel; and the five rules mentioned in Article V of Chapter II of this Second Part: all of these will be pasted upon heavy backs or framed.

Finally, there will be in the classroom of the writers a little bell, which will be rung for the school exercises.

The Twelve Virtues of a Good Teacher

Seriousness, Silence, Humility, Prudence, Wisdom, Patience, Restraint, Gentleness, Zeal, Watchfulness, Piety, and Generosity.

INDEX

INDEX

INDEX

INDEX

M

Maillefer, Mme de, 6

Manual of Prayers, 54, 58, 59, 60, 111, 113, 122, 127, 209

Manuscripts, reading of, 67, 82 f., 88

Martinique, college in, 29

Mass, attendance at, 112, 117 ff., 126, 168, 205, 206, 209, 212

  manner of serving, 57 f.

  responses of, 57 ff., 88, 150, 188

Mazarin, Duke de, 15

Meditations, 112, 148

Miserere, psalm, 112, 139, 215

Mission of the Institute, 22

Mobilization in 1914, 34

Models for writing, 86 f., 90

Moral instruction, 76, 81, 87, 112 f., 119, 132 f., 137, 171, 209

Morning prayers, 59, 112

Mother house, at St. Yon, 27

  in Lembecq-les-Hal, 33

  in Lyons, 31

  in Paris, 32

Multiplication, 105, 106, 107

Mysteries, 128, 129, 130

  pictures of the, 160

N

Napoleon I, 31

National Convention, 15

New pupils, 181, 183

New Testament, 53, 87

Normal schools, 15, 32

Novitiate, at St. Yon, 27

  first, 14

  in Avignon, 25

  in Paris, 18

Numerals, 78 f.

  Arabic, 79

  charts of, 227

  Roman, 79

Nyel, Adrien, 6 f.

O

Oath of submission to civil constitution of the clergy, 30

Obscenity, 176

O Domina mea, invocation, 141

Offertory, at Mass, 126

Oratorians, 40

Order, in church, 120 ff., 168, 175, 177, 184

  in school, 50 ff., 64, 100, 115 f., 142 ff., 148 f., 154, 162, 197

  on streets, 50, 118 f., 125, 140 f., 218

INDEX

INDEX

INDEX

INDEX

INDEX